The Adventures of **Pete** *and* **Cody**

by

Dekota R. Cagle

The Adventures of Pete and Cody
By Dekota R. Cagle

Published by   Bright Virtue Publishing
                 www.bright-virtue.com

Printed in the United States of America
2013 first edition

ISBN-13: 978-0615769721
Copyright ©2013 by Dekota R. Cagle

Edited by Damon T. Cagle

All rights reserved. No part of this book may be reproduced or transmitted in any form or by any means, electronic or mechanical, including photocopying and recording, or by any information storage and retrieval system, without permission in writing from the publisher. Initial inquiry may be sent to admin@bright-virtue.com.

TABLE OF CONTENTS

Bows and Arrows..1
The Cows are Out......................................6
The Launching of Fat Jack........................12
The Boots...19
The Silo..26
The Plague...32
Hot Water..38
Cottonmouth..44
Mary and the Skunk..............................50
The Preacher's Poultice..........................60
How to Stop the Preacher......................69
The Science Lesson................................75
The Wrestler..81
The Watermelon....................................84
Red's Fish...103
Georgie the Parrot...............................112
The Lake House...................................122
Sneaking Out.......................................145
Blind Sections......................................152
Hitchhiking..158

Dedication

This book is dedicated to
Albert "Red" Reding
1906-1984

His heart was far too big to put into a book.

He taught me a good work ethic and that it takes patience and hard work to really succeed. You don't quit just because things get tough.

He taught me to keep my faith in God, and that one needs food for the soul as well as the body.

He taught me that you need a good sense of humor in life. You must be able to laugh at yourself before you can laugh at others.

He taught me that by simply being there, you can have a powerful effect on a person's life.

He taught me that there are certain consequences for one's actions—some good and some bad. But, in the end, justice will be served.

Thanks, Red, for all your guidance.

Cody

Disclaimer

The stories in this book are being recounted for the purpose of humor only, and not as a model of behavior. Some of the shenanigans you will read about in this book are dangerous or even illegal. Others are just plain stupid. Don't try any of these things yourself.

Foreword

Over the years, I've used storytelling and writing as a way to relieve stress. I've always been able to laugh at my own circumstances and find some humor in almost everything that has happened to me. Among the stories that I enjoy telling are those of my experiences growing up in western Oklahoma in the late 1950s and early 1960s.

Originally, I began writing the stories included in this book as a joke for a friend of mine. Though it may defy belief, the stories in this book are not a collection of anecdotes that I heard elsewhere or simply made up. Rather, they are the actual events of my life, as honestly as I can recall them. I have found the truth to be genuinely more entertaining than fiction. The people in this book are real individuals that I have personally known. The "Pete" you will encounter in the following pages is William Peter Reding, my best friend from childhood. And all of these events happened in and around my childhood home of Geary, Oklahoma.

At one point, Pete and I both might have been (and probably were) referred to as "juvenile delinquents," though we were never actually adjudicated in a court of law. You might get that idea yourself from reading these stories. Thankfully, over the years Pete and I received an abundance of guidance from his parents and mine, and we eventually turned into hard-working, law-abiding citizens. But during my childhood I was blessed to enjoy a great deal of fun and mischief, and I think my entire life afterward was shaped by these events.

I hope that whoever reads these stories will find as much humor, excitement, and adventure reading them as I did living them.

Dekota R. "Cody" Cagle

❧Bows and Arrows❧

The first time I remember seeing Pete was when I was about six years old. He had his big black-rimmed glasses on. They looked like something Buddy Holly might have worn. The lenses were as thick as the bottom of an old glass soda bottle. I didn't know it at the time, but without his glasses he couldn't see himself in the mirror at a distance of ten feet.

Pete was very athletic, outgoing, and one of the funniest people I have ever known. He and I spent almost all of the first twenty years of our lives together. We probably would have been together longer, except that when Pete and I went to take our physicals for the military, I passed and Pete didn't.

Geary, Oklahoma, where we lived, was a farm town of fewer than a thousand people, almost all of whom made their living by some type of agriculture. I lived on the edge of town and Pete lived on a dairy farm out in the country. But, a few years after we started hanging out together, our grandmothers both moved into town and lived only a block apart. So, when Pete came into town to stay at his grandmother's house, we usually spent the better part of our time together.

One summer day while I was staying at my grandmother's house, Pete showed up. He was holding a new orange fiberglass bow and five arrows that he had gotten for his birthday. We were about ten years old. Naturally, we both wanted to try out the new bow, but after shooting cardboard boxes for a few minutes we found that it was not interesting enough. We decided we needed more of a challenge and started looking for live targets like squirrels and rabbits in the canyon behind my grandmother's house.

Unfortunately, there wasn't a lot of game in the canyon and we were soon bored again. We decided to return to my grandmother's house and climb up on top of the chicken coop to watch for sparrows to light in a big mulberry tree that grew next to the coop. The sparrows were frequently around the mulberry tree because my grandmother scattered grain out on the ground daily for the chickens.

On top of the chicken coop we waited patiently for the sparrows to show up. Eventually, a few sparrows lit in the mulberry tree, but we quickly learned that a sparrow is a really small target. After a few attempts, and a couple of lost arrows, we decided sparrows wouldn't do either. We still wanted a live target, but we needed something much bigger than a sparrow. To our young minds, it seemed that the only logical choice was one of my grandmother's big, fat, white leghorn hens, which happened to be walking directly below us alongside the barn.

Pete and I took some of the green mulberry leaves from the tree and crumbled them close alongside the barn as food to occupy the hens. Sure enough, it worked. I shot the first arrow, which went straight through the body of one of the hens and pinned it to the ground. We found the ensuing commotion it displayed to be quite entertaining. I gave Pete a turn.

It wasn't until after the third hen had been shot that I began to realize my grandmother knew exactly how many chickens she owned. I became almost nauseated worrying about how to dispose of the dead chickens without her knowing what we had done.

Since it was summertime and wheat harvest was in full swing, Pete and I were quickly able to devise a plan. Our solution was to place the chickens in the middle of the road and make it appear that a wheat truck had run over them. After all, it was common knowledge that my grandmother's chickens would escape the pen and wander all the way to the front of the house to peck at gravel from the road. Thus, a chicken being killed by passing traffic was quite plausible.

Once all three chickens had been laid in the middle of the road, perfectly in single file and so close together that they almost touched each other, Pete and I backed off and evaluated our plot. It looked great to us; it was the perfect ending to a minor problem. But it was at this point that we had our biggest lapse in judgment. We decided that we should be "good Samaritans" and go tell my grandmother about the terrible accident involving a wheat truck running over her chickens. That way we would not only escape punishment, but we would also get big pats on the back for our help.

Pete and I walked to the door and gave a knock. My grandmother answered the door and found herself face-to-face with two boys, bow and arrows in hand, sharing the sad tale of a wheat truck which had run over her chickens.

Now, my grandmother had been around the block a few times. She had grown up as part of a hillbilly family in the Ozarks and outlived three husbands. She dipped snuff and kept a loaded shotgun by the front door. After a short investigation of the chickens in the road, she invited us into her house for what we thought was going to be a thank-you party. But it turned out to be a trap. She had both of us confined within the house behind locked doors with no means of escape. She broke the bow and the arrows, and I thought she might have broken a bone in my upper thigh with a paddle that my dad had made for her for just such an occasion. Then, when Pete and I got home, we got the same treatment from our mothers.

But our brilliance could not be so easily deterred, and this episode marked the opening act of what would be many more adventures together.

꘏The Cows are Out꘏

Pete and I did things together whenever possible. There were times, however, that we would start a project together but only one of us would be available later to suffer the consequences of our "good idea."

On one occasion, we were again in town at our grandmothers' houses and Pete had come over to visit. This was long enough after the incident with the chickens that things had calmed down considerably.

There was an older lady who lived a couple houses down from my grandmother who would visit on a regular basis. Everyone in town referred to the lady as Ma Wilcox. Ma Wilcox had a son who evidently had some extra money, because she was always driving a new car and had what Pete and I considered fancy stuff all throughout her house. When referring to the nice things in her home, Ma Wilcox would always comment, "My son, Herbert, bought this for me."

Well, Herbert had bought Ma Wilcox the first television that Pete and I had ever seen. And that day we were invited to watch the new television.

We were in total awe. It had three channels and could get all kinds of shows and movies. Our favorite show quickly became *Tarzan*, which aired every Saturday morning. It didn't take long for our mothers and grandmothers to figure out that television was a great babysitter. Pete and I would stay glued to the television as long as any cowboy or Tarzan movie was available.

One day, during one of the Tarzan movies, there was a scene in which some of the safari hunters and their guides built what they called an "elephant trap." Pete and I were fascinated by how the men dug a huge hole about ten feet deep and fifteen feet across and covered it with bamboo sticks and large leaves. Their plan was that, when an elephant came lumbering down the trail, it would fall off into the pit and would not be able to climb back out. When the guides checked the trap the next day, the elephant was just sitting there in the bottom of the pit.

As I sat on Ma Wilcox's couch watching this, I nudged Pete. "Hey, I've got an idea!"

Pete looked at me. "What's your idea?"

"You know how we are always trying to catch those rabbits?" I began.

Pete and I had literally spent hours on some days with our BB guns, trying to catch (or shoot) the cottontail rabbits that hid under piles of wooden fence posts behind the barn at my house. The problem that we had encountered was that whenever we would finally dig one of the rabbits out of a pile, it would simply run at full speed down the trail to the next pile and escape. This had infuriated Pete and me. In all the innumerable times we had dug out rabbits, neither of us had ever actually gotten off a shot at any of them. They were just too fast.

I continued telling Pete my idea. I told him that we needed to dig a pit in the trail that connected the two biggest piles of posts. When the rabbit ran down the trail between them it would fall into the elephant trap and we would finally catch it. Pete became extremely excited and congratulated me on what a great plan I had formulated.

The next day we put our project into action. We spent the full day with an old army shovel taking turns digging the elephant trap. The hole we proudly managed to dig was about three feet square on the top and about four feet deep. Now, how could we conceal it? We ran to the house and rummaged through the cabinet drawers until we found some old brown paper grocery sacks, which we cut lengthwise in half.

After lying some very thin slats of old lumber across the pit, we carefully placed the grocery sacks to cover them and thus completely hide the four-foot hole. We sprinkled grass and red Oklahoma dirt across the tops of the grocery sacks until they were perfectly camouflaged.

When we finished, we admired our creation. As we stood staring, Pete shook his head. "I actually feel sorry for that rabbit," he said. "He won't have a chance."

Well, neither Pete nor I ever had a problem entertaining ourselves. It had taken us the whole day to dig the pit and cover it. Now we were eager to start the next day digging rabbits out from under the piles of fence posts and watching them run helplessly and unknowingly into our trap.

But, for some reason, Pete and I got tied up with chores the next day and didn't get to do the rabbit safari. Actually, about three days passed after we had dug the trap and camouflaged it.

My mother had a friend named Elsie who used to come and visit on occasion. Elsie had two boys that were younger than me, and I always had to keep them outside and entertain them while the women stayed in the house and gossiped.

The two boys and I were outside playing in the front yard that day. My mother and Elsie were sitting on the front porch drinking iced tea. Suddenly, my older brother appeared from around the north side of the house and gave the alarm call. "The cows are out!" he hollered. "And they're heading toward the blackjacks!"

It would mean a lot of trouble if the cattle actually made it to the blackjack trees. Getting them out of the trees was practically impossible. Everyone jumped up and started to the barn to put the calves back into the pens before they made it to the woods.

Out back, everyone circled the cattle and started easing them back into the pens. As usual, one of the calves didn't want to go back into the pen. It made a run to escape out into the wider pasture where the blackjack trees were located.

Elsie happened to be closest to the escaping calf, but she would need to hurry to head it off. I was impressed at the blazing speed Elsie exhibited for a lady of her age. She was in a dead run, head laid back, legs churning, as she raced across the pasture to head off the calf.

Then, suddenly, she was gone. She disappeared into a cloud of red dust and grass clippings. She had found the elephant trap! At the time, I actually found it rather amusing to see her disappear into the dust cloud. I stood there laughing to myself, thinking, "That was the coolest thing I have ever seen!" The trap Pete and I had constructed worked to perfection.

Unfortunately, the fall into the trap had slammed Elsie face-first into the ground and had broken her glasses and bloodied her nose. While everyone stared in disbelief and tried to figure out what had happened, I turned and started walking toward the blackjacks to escape with the calf. As my pace quickened I looked back at my mother and saw on her face that she had realized what I had done. She picked up the closest object she could find to whack me with and headed in my direction. It was a dried cedar limb from the post piles. Besides escaping, my only thought was, "How does she know my brother didn't build that trap?"

⁂The Launching of Fat Jack⁂

On the North Canadian River about five miles northeast of Geary there was a swimming hole that every kid in the surrounding communities would visit on Saturday or on Sunday afternoon after church. We called it the "Rock Hole." It was a stretch of water on the river that flowed straight east into a solid clay rock bank about twenty-five feet high. The water striking the east bank of the river made a huge whirlpool as the river turned south. The sharp turn in the river dug the sand from the bottom and made a perfect large swimming pool about thirty yards across in every direction. The water would sometimes be as much as fifteen feet deep. As far as I know, this hole of water is still there today. It is located straight south of Jesse Chisholm's gravesite.

On one particular Saturday a large group of kids had gathered at the Rock Hole, including the boys whose dad owned the property.

Pete and I were among the large group of kids. We were all swimming and playing in the river having a grand summer day.

A short time later we looked down the river to see all of the Chambless boys coming down the river bank. There were Kenny, Gene, Earl, Lester, Clyde, and Carl James. All of the boys had managed to get aboard one little Model A Ford tractor and had driven three miles to the Rock Hole to swim and fish. I was about ten years old at the time and somewhere in the neighborhood of sixty pounds.

The Chambless boys were much older than almost everyone there swimming that day. I think their real intent was to come to the river and noodle for catfish because they were all known to be good noodlers. At any rate, while we all swam they whooped and hollered, and splashed all the younger kids.

With the old Ford tractor parked on the sand bank, the Chambless boys took a break up in the shade next to it, resting from their harassment of all of us younger kids.

As we kept an eye on the Chambless boys, Clyde, who was next to Carl James in age, came from out of the trees with an old tractor inner tube. They began to have a conversation among themselves and soon we saw one of the boys produce a large pocket knife and begin to cut on the old tractor inner tube. Soon they had cut the tube completely apart. Then they took the tube and sliced it down the middle to make what looked like a large rubber blanket. We all watched as Kenny, the oldest boy, and Gene, the next oldest, got on the tractor and disappeared for a few minutes. When they returned they had posthole diggers, rope, a chopping ax, and two large cedar corner posts.

They again began to talk among themselves, and shortly after that they began to build what appeared to be a large slingshot. When Pete and I discovered what they were building, we had to get involved.

Soon all the kids were up on the bank with the Chambless boys building a gigantic slingshot. As the construction project was going on they explained their plan of action. They could build this huge slingshot, and then someone could sit inside of the inner tube and be shot out into the river.

The lucky person could sit inside the inner tube and they would pull the rubber sling back using the tractor and shoot the person inside the tube out into the river. It all seemed like a great plan until they got it finished and needed a volunteer. They began to talk among themselves again. They knew my dad really well and they knew me pretty well, so one of the oldest boys said,

"Let's get Cody to ride in it. He's small and tough."

One of the older boys added, "Then we'll know if it works or not. If it does we all can take a ride in it." Seemed like a great plan to me. Or, it did at the time, at least.

As the launch site was being prepared for action, it gave us sufficient time for deeper reflection. All of a sudden, one of the Chambless boys yelled, "Wait! I've got a better idea!"

Well, to put it simply, his plan was to move the launch site from the three-foot-high sand bank up to the twenty-five-foot-high bluff overlooking the river. So, after a thirty minute launch delay, we were all located on the high rock bluff overlooking the Rock Hole in the river.

As the cedar post was being set and the large rubber tube being attached, I was getting coached by Pete and a number of my other friends—the Ogle boys, whose dad owned the place; the Helm boys, who lived farther west of the river than any of us; some of the Moore boys from Calumet, and a number of other bystanders.

The plan was for me to sit inside the inner tube and curl up into a small ball. Then the

Chambless boys would pull the inner tube back with a rope tied to the tractor, and, when the inner tube was nice and tight, they would use the ax to cut the rope while it lay on a large wooden block. By cutting the rope I would be launched out into the river.

I felt a little anxious as I climbed inside the tube. I had faith though, especially because of all the peer pressure I had received during my coaching session. I was doing the right thing.

Just before launch I recalled my mom saying to me one day, "I thank God every day you weren't twins." Then I thought to myself inside the tube, "Well, if I had a twin, at least one of us would survive this."

I can remember to this day how it snapped my body when I left the launch site. Before I knew it I was twenty feet out over the swimming hole. Then, *kersplash*, I hit the water. When I surfaced, everyone on top of the hill was ecstatic at the success of our operation. I felt like a hero as I swam to shore to cheers of praise and excitement.

Well, a few minutes later, I was back on top of the hill as they prepared the launch site for the second rider. A fight almost broke out as kids argued over who was going to ride next. Finally, one of the older Chambless boys picked the next rider. It was "Fat" Jack. Fat Jack was in the same room at school as Pete and I. But Jack was much larger physically than both of us put together, as one might guess by his nickname. I always liked him because it was really easy to get him laughing in the classroom at school. Because of me, he had been escorted down the hall to the principal's office on more than one occasion.

It took a little more coaching and a lot of coaxing to get Fat Jack inside the inner tube. When he was firmly inside he gave the signal that he was ready to be launched. They began to pull the tube back with the tractor, and it became tighter and tighter as they pulled.

One of the Chambless boys kept saying, "He's a lot bigger than Cody; keep pulling." Because of Jack's weight, they decided it best to stretch the tube to its very limit.

When Carl James cut the rope it sent Fat Jack flying like an astronaut. He flew up into the air and out over the swimming hole. Unfortunately, he didn't stop there. He traveled in an arc right over the pool. As Pete later commented, he looked like a big white whale with his arms and legs thrashing around as if he were trying to fly.

The Chambless boys had launched Jack, not into the river, but all the way across it and onto the sandbar on the far side, where he landed with a giant thud.

We later learned the extent of his injuries. It had broken both Jack's wrists when he hit the ground on the other side.

After this, the NASA swimming party was quickly dispersed. The Chambless boys disappeared back down the river on the tractor. Jack went to the doctor. And Pete and I went home with a case of selective amnesia. We couldn't recall a single thing out of the ordinary that had happened that day that our parents might need to know about. They found out later, of course. But not from us.

❧The Boots❧

As Pete and I got older we were required to work what we felt was an excessive amount. We were either in the hayfields moving alfalfa hay with my father or helping Pete's father, Red, milk cows. At the beginning, Red only milked four cows and sold the milk and cream in town at the market. Later on, in the early 1960s, he started milking cows commercially. At one point we were milking about thirty cows twice a day. I quickly learned that milking cows was a hard job. You milk twice a day at six in the morning and at six in the evening, every day with no days off.

During my teen years when I was employed milking cows, I basically lived at Pete's house. During the time between milking, Pete and I would spend as much time as we could outdoors. We would fish all summer and hunt all fall and winter. School was our only interference.

On one of our fall outings in late September, Pete and I were hunting squirrels along the North Canadian River. The area where we were hunting was an old oxbow lake surrounded by canyons filled with cottonwood and black walnut trees.

We hadn't had a lot of success that day and were headed back to the truck when we topped a small hill that overlooked a flooded grass flat that ran along the oxbow. The season being fall, the first flights of teal ducks had made their way south. They had established roosting sites and feeding areas all along the Canadian River. What Pete and I saw as we topped the hill was roughly a two-acre pothole of water in the grass flat that was completely covered with teal ducks.

We quickly made a plan to rush home, retrieve our shotguns, return to the pothole, shoot some ducks, and return home before milking time.

Pete and I went home and hurriedly gathered all the equipment we would need for the duck hunt. What I didn't know at the time was that Pete had changed his shoes. He had, for some reason still unknown to me, put on a pair of new, name-brand, insulated, kangaroo-skin boots belonging to his father.

Only one day before our duck hunt, Red had shown us the new boots that he had just purchased for sixty dollars. That was an enormous amount of money. For perspective, Red was paying Pete and me two dollars a week for milking. To say that he was proud of his purchase would be a massive understatement. He had gone on and on about how warm and comfortable the boots would be while walking on the cold, wet, cement floor of the old milk barn during the coming months of winter.

When Pete and I arrived back at the slough, we prepared our sneak attack on the helpless ducks. We decided to crawl up to the swampy hole from two separate directions and catch the ducks in a crossfire of lead pellets. However, shortly after we had separated, I could see a flaw in our plan because I found myself wading knee-deep through thick, black, tarry mud. It was really taking its toll on me. There was no way to maneuver without bogging down to my knees. And if I tried to bend over and crawl, I would have had to submerge both hands, along with the shotgun, in the mud in order to move at all. I guessed Pete was having the same experience.

When we finally scared the ducks into flight, we both emptied our guns shooting at them. After the barrage of pellets, we surveyed the damage and could only find one duck, and it was shamefully small.

Once we retrieved our prized duck, we started making our way back to the truck so that we could be home by milking time. It was on the way back to the truck that I noticed something different about Pete's footwear. I could hear wet, squishing sounds as we walked. Upon closer examination, I found that Pete was wearing Red's new kangaroo-skin boots. They were dripping wet and lathered in smelly, black mud as thick as gumbo. We both stopped in the roadway and attempted to scrape the mud from the boots, but it was futile. We decided to rush home as fast as possible and clean the boots before milking time.

We slid into the yard in the truck and Pete took the boots out behind the house. He sprayed them with the water hose while attempting to scrape off the mud with a butter knife from the kitchen. Meanwhile, I cleaned the duck.

It took Pete a while, but he finally got the boots cleaned up sufficiently that we thought they could pass Red's inspection. But we needed to dry them out quickly. So, we took them out to the milk barn and placed them on top of an old open-flame propane heater that was used to heat the barn.

Pete turned the burner up and placed the kangaroo-skin boots on top of the stove. It was our intention to dry the boots quickly and return them to the house without Red ever knowing they were gone. Thus, our crime would be forever concealed.

We walked back to the house, smirking at each other in our genius. A bit later, it seemed like our scheme would work to perfection, until…suddenly, from down the hallway inside the house came a blood-curdling scream: "The barn is on fire!"

The thunder of footsteps echoed down the hallway as Red raced toward the back. As he shot out the door, his voice could be heard repeating, "The barn is on fire! The barn is on fire!" He blew through the screen door at full speed and turned toward the milk barn, flying across the yard in a panic.

Pete and I were glued to the window watching Red run toward the barn with one strap of his overalls blowing in the wind behind his left shoulder. Luminescent blue smoke was billowing out from every window in the old barn while we stared in utter disbelief. Quickly, we hurried out of the house and made it to the door of the barn.

We watched silently as Red fanned smoke with his hands, coughed, and scoured the inside of the barn to find the source of the fire. The air smelled of branded rawhide. As we entered the fray, Pete and I both had somehow intuitively guessed the best area of the barn to search for flames. Hurrying through the blue haze, Pete and I spotted the source of the smoke. Unfortunately, Red had found it about the same time we had.

There, on top of the old propane stove, sat a pair of what appeared to be tiny pixie shoes, totally shriveled, with toes turned up into the air. Except for the smoke they were radiating, they reminded me of a pair of elf shoes I had been forced to wear in a May Day program when I was in fourth grade. The bottoms of the boots were red embers and the tops were gray with ashes.

Red picked up the tiny boots between his index finger and thumb, eyeing them in puzzlement. After a few moments of examination, he realized what he was actually holding in his hand were not pixie shoes, but his own kangaroo-skin boots.

In the blink of an eye, Red was holding the inch-thick wooden handle of an old milk mop and running out of the smoke-filled barn after Pete and me. I could envision my cold, bludgeoned body lying on the ground and Red standing over me laughing evilly.

When he cleared the barn door, mop handle in hand, Pete and I ran in opposite directions. Luckily for us, the smoke in the barn had made Red's eyes tear up and clouded his vision. His eyes were watering so badly that he couldn't see which one of us was closest.

I attribute my escape to my youth and my simply being faster than Red. Still, during the pursuit I heard words that I had never heard before and wouldn't learn the meaning of until much later in life.

After our escape, Pete and I made it to a friend's house about a mile away. We refused to go home until we were completely assured by Mary, Pete's mother, that we would not be shot on sight or beaten to death.

Incidentally, Pete and I milked cows for the next two years for free.

❧The Silo❧

Looking back, it seems that Pete and I would have at least one major lapse in judgment a year. Sometimes, as fate would have it, we would have two or three. I generally blamed Pete for what had occurred during our setbacks. When caught, my excuse was always, "It was Pete's idea." Sometimes that worked. Sometimes it didn't.

It is not unusual for summers in Oklahoma to be unbearably hot and dry. Pete and I were about fourteen years old and we were experiencing one of those extreme summers. All of the cattle pasture had dried up from the heat, and we were kept busy feeding huge amounts of ground feed to the cows so that we could keep up with the milk quota. The effects of the heat also made all of the rats and mice that normally stayed in the pastures seek food and shelter elsewhere.

One of the places that all these rats and mice chose to take up residence was in an old, circle-shaped brick pit that was the remains of where a grain silo had once stood. It was about twenty-five steps from the back of Red's milk barn. This pit was made of hollow red bricks and provided a perfect refuge for all the rats and mice that had come in from the fields.

The top of the old silo had been broken off previously by a tornado that had come sweeping by the house. What the tornado had left was an outer ring of brick standing about three feet above the ground. In the center of the bricks was a hole that was about ten feet across and twelve feet deep. Over the years, it had become a refuse pit. People had thrown wooden boards, baling wire, moldy hay, burlap feed sacks, and anything else considered farm waste into the silo.

I think Red's ultimate intention was to someday bulldoze the old silo down, fill in the hole, and level the whole area. But, for now, the silo pit had become a safe haven for every field rat and mouse for miles around. And the rodents had become dependent upon cattle feed as their main source of food. Late at night the little varmints were getting into the feed that we were putting out for the cattle. On top of that, they had managed to tunnel inside the main feed bins where we stored the rest of the feed inside the wooden granaries.

We were almost finished milking one evening when Red told Pete and me to go get a full can of diesel fuel, which, to Pete and me, meant five gallons. He told us that once we had gotten the fuel we were to pour it on the old boards and rotten hay in the silo pit and set it on fire. This would take care of all the rats and mice living in the silo that had been eating the cattle feed.

Now, this was a dream come true for Pete and me. We had experimented with flammable materials before and were all too excited with this new chore. While jogging to get the fuel can, we discussed how cool it was going to be to get to blow up all the rats and mice.

We found the five-gallon can and had started to fill it at the main fuel tank. We had it about half full when Pete had a better idea. Rather than tire ourselves carrying a full can of diesel fuel all the way back out to the milk barn, we would take the old green pickup truck and simply drive up beside the silo. Once there, we would pump a little diesel down into the pit from the two-hundred-fifty-gallon fuel tank that sat in the back of the truck.

Arriving at the silo in the fuel truck, we hung the hose over the side of the red brick wall and started pumping. After just a few minutes, we started to notice lots of rats and mice scurrying around deep in the belly of the old silo. It was somewhere around this point that we lost our minds. We decided that if a little bit of fuel could make the rats and mice run around gasping for air, then a *lot* of fuel would accomplish that much more. So, Pete and I spent the next ten minutes pumping fuel down inside the old silo from the tank in the back of the truck. By this time, it had been about half an hour since we had received the orders from Red to burn out the silo.

When we finally got our wits about us and determined that we had pumped enough fuel into the silo, we both jumped into the truck and moved it about a hundred yards away to a spot on the side of a small hill overlooking the milk barn. As we pulled away, we noticed that the diesel fuel had already begun to atomize and the air was becoming saturated with the smell of its fumes.

Pete and I had parked the truck and were arguing about who would get the honor of striking the first match to roast all those rats, when we looked up and saw Red coming from the milk barn. He was headed toward the silo with what appeared to be a small coffee can. We later learned that this coffee can held about two or three cups of diesel and had been what he meant when he had told us to get a "can of diesel." We also later learned that he had not seen Pete and me pull the truck alongside the silo and pump it full of fuel. Moreover, he was evidently upwind from the pit and couldn't smell the fumes that filled the air.

Pete and I watched helplessly from the hill as Red walked to the edge of the old silo and poured his tiny can of fuel down inside. He took two steps back, lit a match, and pitched it into the silo.

BOOOOOM! The next thing we saw was a huge fireball that blew straight up and about a hundred feet in all directions. The explosion sent Red hurling through the air and slammed him against the wall of the milk barn. Millions of pieces of red brick and flaming hay scattered over an area of about ten acres. Having later served in Vietnam, I can only compare it to a five-hundred-pound napalm bomb.

Pete and I stomped out fires as we made our way down the hill to Red, who was lying against the barn. We looked for burns on his body. The smell of singed hair filled the air. When he finally opened his eyes, I was immediately reminded of the scene from the movie *The Ten Commandments* in which Moses descends the mountain and meets Joshua, who exclaims, "He has seen the face of God!"

The flash from the explosion had burned all the hair off of Red's arms and most of the hair from his face. The hair on his head, normally peppered gray, was now twisted and orange. But, as he slowly regained awareness, I knew the deep crimson color beginning to flood his cheeks was not from the explosion.

When he finally made it to his feet, I began hearing those strange words again. He started with, "I'm gonna kill you two ignorant little…"

I knew from past experience not to be within arm's length once Red gained full consciousness. Still shouting, Red disappeared inside the barn. Pete and I knew he was looking for the mop handle, so we ran.

As we topped the hill to the west of the house, Pete said, "I hope he doesn't find where we hid the shotgun when he gets back from the doctor."

We ran the full mile to our friend's house. His mother could tell something wasn't right by the looks on our faces. She shook her head. "What have you two boys done now? Maybe I should call Mary."

Pete and I remained silent.

≈The Plague≈

Pete and I were both required to attend church regularly. I guess our parents hoped that God would intervene in our lives, since no one else seemed to be having any luck. This was the same summer that we had all the rats come to the silo. We were forced to attend a small, country church about two miles southeast of Pete's house. On Sunday afternoons after church, most of the conversations in the church yard would usually be about rats. Everyone was complaining about the rats coming into their houses and granaries and would talk about what could be done to relieve the problem. Needless to say, the story of Red and the diesel had gotten out, so no one was in a hurry to have Pete and me come over and cure their rat problems.

Late one Saturday while Pete and I were moving some square hay bales from a barn that was located on a small hill above the milk barn, we came across a big, black opossum. Now, most opossums are a light-grayish color with black, shiny ears. But this particular opossum was totally black and looked as if it had been covered at one time with lots of fleas. I say this because most of its hair was gone, and what remained was less than a quarter of an inch long. All this gave the opossum more of the appearance of a giant, mangy rat than an opossum. Pete and I captured the opossum alive and stuffed it into a large burlap bag which we threw into the back of the truck to await our decision about what to do with it.

After we finished feeding the milk cows, we sat down on the tailgate of the truck and talked about what we could do with the opossum that would be funny. Since the next day was Sunday, and since neither of us really liked church or the preacher, we came up with a plan.

We thought that if we took the opossum over to the church and turned it loose inside, someone would see it and think that it was a rat. The news would spread and everyone would think that the church had become infested with rats and cancel the service. This would leave Pete and me free to go fishing.

Later that night, we walked the two miles to the church and turned the opossum loose inside. We laughed all the way home at what we thought would happen. Back home, we decided to plant a few seeds of fear. We got on the old party-line phone and started to call all our friends, and anyone else we could think of, and tell them of a deadly outbreak of the plague that was spreading through the countryside because of all the rats and the fleas that they carried.

Pete and I both were fully aware that the two old maids, Miss Margaret and Miss Pearl, who lived two miles north, would be listening to all of our conversations on the phone. They had ratted us out before to Red and Mary over some of the things we had said to our friends over the phone while they had been listening.

The tiny church where we had released the opossum consisted of only one room where all the pews were located. There were about ten rows of pews on each side of the main aisle that led forward to the pulpit. The stage was one step up from the main floor. On it stood a tall wooden pulpit which was firmly attached to the solid wood floor. This is where the preacher stood to do his preaching.

Sometimes when he was preaching, the preacher would get on what Pete called a "holy roll," marching up and down the aisle bellowing forth fire and brimstone. On most of the trips down the aisle, his arms would be flailing about, and it seemed as if he would be looking directly at Pete and me.

The next morning, we were up early trying to overhear any conversations about large, flea-covered rats that had taken over the church. We even resorted to eavesdropping on the phone like Margaret and Pearl. In the past, Pete and I had gotten some pretty good gossip from the phone lines ourselves. Sometimes the party line phone would be our only source of contact with the outside world. But, today, there was no news about rats or the plague and it was getting close to church time. We both sat and talked about what could have happened to the opossum. We discussed all of the possible means of escape from the church, but couldn't come up with any ideas on how it might have gotten out.

Later, as we followed Red and Mary into the church, we scanned every nook and cranny hoping to yell, "It's a rat with the plague! Run for your lives!" But everything inside the church that morning seemed abnormally quiet. There seemed to be a real presence of the Lord that day.

We were all seated, and everything seemed to be going as usual, but Pete and I were still scanning the darkest corners for any movement. We had made it almost through the entire sermon with no opossum sightings. It seemed that all our efforts had been in vain.

Previously, Pete had brought it to my attention that the preacher used inordinate amounts of

"Oh God's" and "Oh Lord's" while he was waving and preaching. We had made it a game to count the number of times he said "Oh God," and we would get tickled and start laughing uncontrollably during church.

Well, on this particular Sunday the preacher was right in the middle of his "Oh God" sermon from the pulpit, when he leaned back with arms outstretched and head tilted back toward heaven and screamed, "Oh God…what a rat!"

The opossum had somehow managed to climb up one of the large wooden beams leading from the floor to the roof, and was now sitting on a rafter directly above the pulpit where the preacher was preaching. I guess the preacher's scream had scared the opossum, because upon hearing his voice, the opossum scrambled down one of the beams coming from the rafter and scurried across the floor and down the main aisle leading to the doorway, the only exit from the church.

From where I was sitting in the back row, I couldn't tell whether it was Miss Margaret or Miss Pearl that made it over the front pew first. After all, they were twins dressed in identical flowery dresses. Up close they were easier to identify because Miss Pearl had a mustache.

The opossum had no more than touched the floor when Pete jumped up on his pew and yelled at the top of his voice the line that he had been saving for almost an hour: "That rat's got the plague! Run for your lives!"

Pete's yelling emptied the church. I was standing on the back pew with Pete watching all the action. Miss Margaret and Miss Pearl made their escape, clawing their way over a pile of people that were jammed in the doorway.

When the stampede started, there were lots of screams from the women and scrambling from the men. But I couldn't fully enjoy the spectacle, because I could see Red standing atop the front pew staring directly back at Pete and me. I was beginning to get that sick feeling in my stomach, knowing that Pete and I were going to have to pay for our sins at some point.

Pete and I both cleared the tangled mass of bodies in the doorway and jogged away from the church with Red and the preacher close behind.

"Keep running!" I urged Pete. "They won't last a mile!"

That summer, Pete and I got an abundance of exercise, especially from running.

❧Hot Water☙

One day in late August, Red had sent us to the milk barn to clean out the milk tanks. The milk truck would come like clockwork at noon every third day to pick up all the milk that was in the thousand-gallon stainless steel tanks. After the truck drained the tanks, it was our job to boil large buckets of water on the propane heater and sterilize all equipment both inside and out.

On this particular afternoon, it was about a hundred degrees outside. That meant that in the milk barn, where we were working, it had to have been at least a hundred and fifteen degrees. While cleaning the large metal syringes that were used to give shots to the cows, Pete filled one of them with the cool, fresh water that we were using to rinse the equipment with after sterilizing it. Once he had the syringe full, he caught me not looking and sprayed me on my shirtless back. Being sprayed with cool well-water was quite a shock, but it also felt good in the unbearable heat.

Immediately, we were disengaged from our work and playing, shooting each other with cool water from the syringes. Luckily, it didn't matter where we sprayed water because everything in the barn had to be washed down and thoroughly cleaned. The spraying went on for about fifteen minutes until we got bored. We decided to up the ante a bit. I would stand against one wall and Pete would stand against the other while we took turns spraying each other in the face.

About this time Red came through the door and began to scold us for playing around and not doing our job. After a verbal reprimand, we started back on our chores and Red disappeared into the back to shovel feed into the milking stalls. Religiously, we would start milking at six o'clock and the time was nearing.

Shortly, Red headed off toward the house. We had a somewhat distorted view of him through a glass window on the north side of the barn. We both knew that he was probably headed back for an afternoon nap in front of the water-cooled fan. This freed us up to begin spraying each other with syringes again.

After a few bursts of water from the syringes, Pete made his oft-spoken declaration, "Hey, I've got a good idea!"

He pointed to a hole about one inch in diameter on the east wall of the wooden milk barn very near the door. The hole had been made when

Red had run a copper propane line to a heater that used to sit against that wall.

Pete made the suggestion that one of us go outside and look through the hole while the other would stand inside against the west wall about fifteen feet away. The one inside would then attempt to squirt water into the eye of the one who would be looking through the hole from the outside.

I knew Pete well enough to know that there might be more to the plan than he was letting me in on. I therefore suggested that he be the first one to go outside and look through the hole. He agreed, and outside he bounced and quickly placed one eye up against the wooden circle, looking across the barn floor at me standing against the opposite wall.

My first blast of water wasn't very accurate because of the distance. On the second shot, I pushed the syringe with much greater vigor. The resulting pressure caused the stream to be a lot more powerful and a lot more accurate. Thus, I managed to get a full blast of water right into Pete's eye. After the shot, I could hear him outside laughing and yelling. Suddenly, he burst through the door and shouted, "Man, that's cool! You can see the water coming, and all you have to do is close your eye."

On my turn, I discovered that Pete was right about it looking cool. I could see a large stream of water hurling toward my eye, but, of course, the blink of my eye was quicker than the shooting water. Because of this, neither of us was particularly worried about actually having water shot directly into our eyes. Interestingly, this was my first experience in learning that people have a dominant eye.

After about eight or ten turns, we started to get bored again, and we knew it wouldn't be long until it was time to milk. Realizing that we needed to finish our chores before milking time, I suggested that Pete and I each take one more turn and then return to work. He jumped at my offer and said that he would be the first to go outside. I took my turn, finished my shot, and met Pete at the door, handing him the syringe as I headed outside. Placing my eye over the hole I looked across the room but could not see Pete. I yelled at him through the wall asking what he was doing and why it was taking so long to fill the syringe.

"Wait just a second!" he shouted back at me.

I still had my eye against the hole looking for Pete when I felt a hand grasp my shoulder. I turned around and found myself face-to-face with Red. He furrowed his brow. "Boy, what are you looking at in that hole?" He pulled me away from the wall, leaned forward, and stuck his eye against the round, wooden hole to look inside.

Meanwhile, quite unknown to me, Pete had come up with the brilliant idea of filling the syringe not with the cool well-water that we had been shooting, but instead with the scalding hot soapy water that we had been using to clean the tanks. Moreover, to ensure that I didn't have time to blink, he had moved to a distance of only about six inches from the wall.

As soon as Red placed his eye against the hole, he was shot full force directly in the eye with a stream of scalding hot water. He immediately fell back from the hole, screaming and yelling and clutching at his right eye with both hands. I could hear Pete in the barn laughing, thinking that he had just shot me in the eye with hot, soapy water. But it wasn't long before he realized that the thundering voice he heard on the other side of the wall was not mine. It was only then that Pete realized that he had shot Red in the eye, and not me.

As usual, since I was closest, I was the first target of Red's rage. He tried to grab me but missed. I think in his rage and confusion, he couldn't decide whether to grab me and start punching or just punch.

At any rate, I was able to escape across the yard and head east to the trees across the road. Looking back over my shoulder, I could see Pete heading west over the big sandy hill behind the barn. "How thoughtless of him not to even check out the damage he had done to his dad's eye," I thought.

Over the next hour or so, I would venture out to the edge of the trees and scan the area around the house and barn. I could see Red pacing restlessly between them, a mop handle in his hand and an x-shaped patch that he had made from white tape over his eye.

I stayed in the trees as long as I could, but later I could hear Red calling the cows. It was milking time and I would have to go back and face the consequences. As I slowly walked back to the milk barn, I rehearsed my confession, especially the part where it had all been Pete's idea.

ઠ•Cottonmouth•ઠ

During the summer months, Pete and I would spend enormous amounts of time on the North Canadian River, fishing and swimming. During our many trips, we learned to catch fish with our hands. This sport, often referred to as "noodling," has steadily gained popularity in Oklahoma, and Pete and I both became very proficient in the skill. We commonly showed up at the house with one or two catfish weighing twenty pounds or more. Red was always impressed with the number and size of the fish that we caught with our hands.

All summer, we would continually invite Red to accompany us on one of our noodling trips. He would always decline the offers because he was deathly afraid of snakes. Red had heard all the stories of snakes, beavers, snapping turtles, and many other horrific dangers of noodling for catfish.

We constantly assured him that such dangers were always overstated and that there would be no real threat to his life if he came with us. Pete and I kept telling him that we really wanted him to come and watch while we caught a big fish with our hands and that he needn't even get in the water. After many invitations, we eventually talked Red into making a trip with us to the river so that he could observe.

After we completed our milking chores, Pete and I discussed which part of the river would be the best area to find a big catfish for the following day's trip with Red. That was when one of Pete's notoriously good ideas came to his mind.

"Hey, you know what would be funny?" asked Pete.

"What?" I asked, as usual.

Once Pete had told me his plan, I agreed that it would indeed be really funny.

Later that night, Pete and I drove down to what everyone called the "Old Slough," which was the oxbow lake that joined the river. It had once been the main river channel until, over the years, the river had changed course. It was full of downed timber…and hoards of snakes.

Once at the Old Slough, we caught the first harmless brown water snake we could find and put it into a burlap sack. When we arrived back at the house we put the sack, with the snake inside, in the deep freeze which was out back in the shed. The next day when we left to take Red fishing, we took the burlap sack with us.

On our fishing trips, we usually took a small johnboat and floated down the river to large logjams or root-covered banks—places where we thought we might find catfish. When we placed the small boat in the river that day, we put the rolled-up burlap sack into the back of the boat. Since Red had never gone with us before, he didn't know that we usually put the catfish on long nylon stringers rather than in burlap sacks.

After about an hour of fishing with no luck, I secretly motioned to Pete that it was time to put our plan into action. We figured that the snake had plenty of time to thaw out after being in the freezer all night. We paddled the boat to a group of large willow trees that hung over the river. The banks here were covered in a tangle of tree roots. It looked more like a good home for a big cottonmouth water moccasin snake than for a catfish. Cottonmouths were known and feared by locals as one of the few poisonous species native to that part of the state.

As we had traveled down the river in the boat, Pete and I had been careful to point out to Red each of the many large snakes that were lying on the tops of the brush piles or lying in root clumps along the clay-covered banks. We had done this to give him the correct mindset for what was about to happen.

As the boat slowed along the river's edge, Pete and I climbed out and slid off into the water, which was about chest deep. I began to feel under the root bank with a stick and along a large log that lay half-submerged beneath the water.

After a while, Pete gave me the signal. Loud enough for Red to hear, I told Pete to get the sack because there was a nice-sized catfish lying in a hole underneath the bank. Previously, I had made the remark to Red that I could smell the scent of a cottonmouth and told him to keep his eyes peeled for a snake.

There was, of course, no odor. But it is true that the snakes emit a foul smell if disturbed from their sunning activities. Red was an old-school rod-and-reel fisherman who had fished all over the state and had encountered these snakes before. He knew exactly what I was talking about when I told him of the snake's scent. I noticed him sniffing the air, trying to get a whiff of it. His face became anxious and he had a white-knuckle grip clamped firmly to the edge of the boat.

When Pete approached me with the sack, I slowly submerged myself under the water as if I were looking for a fish. When I came up, Pete moved over to my side, holding the burlap sack in his hands. We both started to feel around the root-covered bank and beneath the log, telling Red that we were trying to find the exact position of the fish so we could catch it.

In reality, we were taking the water snake out of the burlap sack. The snake was dead from being frozen all night, but had thawed nicely and was now quite limber. Once I found the snake inside the sack, I gripped the back of its head firmly and submerged myself again back beneath the surface. Staying under as long as I could, I began to kick and thrash around under the water, giving the indication that something unusual was happening.

When I exploded to the surface, I had the snake's head planted firmly against my neck as if it had bitten me on the throat. Then, with a blood-curdling scream, I yelled, "Oh, no, it's a cottonmouth!!!" At exactly the same time, I tossed the snake directly at Red, who was still sitting in the boat.

Now, there were a good fifteen feet of open water between the boat and the opposite bank of the river. And, after that, it was ten more feet straight up the river's muddy bank to the top. As the snake left my hand and was travelling through the air toward Red, I could see a look of sheer terror on his face. But amazingly, before the snake ever reached him, he managed to move from a sitting position, directly vertical to a point hanging four feet above the boat in mid-air. He did this without making a single ripple on the water. Once aloft, he turned in mid-air, and made three long strides across the top of the water to the opposite bank. He looked like some type of exotic water bird trying to take off as he skipped across the surface of the river.

On the opposite bank, he clawed his way to the top, yelling a jumble of incomprehensible words. He did all this without getting a single drop of water or speck of mud on his blue-bibbed overalls.

As he disappeared over the river bank and out into the woods, Pete and I laughed hysterically at the result of our plot. We were still standing in the river laughing when we heard Red yell from somewhere out of sight, "When you get out on the bank, I'm gonna kill you two little...!"

Pete and I stayed in the river and floated back to the truck, but stayed clear of the banks for fear of the shadowy figure in the trees that seemed to be carrying a large wooden club.

We didn't come out of the river until after dark. And, when we finally did, we walked all the way back home because Red had taken the truck and left us at the river.

ò Mary and the Skunk ô

It was the middle of January. The weather in Oklahoma is known for extreme swings in temperature. It is not uncommon for a cold front to come through which causes the temperature to drop twenty degrees or more within minutes. When this happens, we call it a "blue northern." There had been just this kind of blue northern cold front that had blown in during the night and the temperature had dropped dramatically in a very short period of time. Pete and I had gotten up in the dark to do our milking chores. When we finished, it was barely daybreak.

We raced to the house from the milk barn to enjoy a huge breakfast that Pete's mother, Mary, had cooked. Mary was a tall, thin lady. She was a wonderful cook, humorous, and an all-around good farm wife. Pete and I were always overly considerate and courteous to her simply for the number of times she had saved our lives from Red.

We finished breakfast, got dressed, and gathered our books for school. The school bus was never very punctual. It might arrive thirty minutes early or thirty minutes late. At any rate, we were sitting in the front room waiting for it to arrive.

This was one of the few times that Pete and I were allowed in the front room. The reason for our general exclusion was that the entire room had been covered with brand new white pile carpet. This carpet had been the talk of the community when it was purchased. Lots of other homes in the area were fortunate just to have some kind of rubber linoleum on the floors. And there were many others that merely had old moisture-warped tongue-and-groove wooden floors, unpolished at that. I guess a carpet of any kind would have been a source of pride for any woman in the community. In fact, Mary's carpet was such a big deal that people would drive fifteen miles from Calumet just to see it.

Pete's dad, Red, had gotten one of the first oil-and-gas leases in western Oklahoma and had taken some of the money to buy the carpet for Mary. Unknown to Red, Pete and I had used the carpet as a wrestling mat once when we were forced to take care of Pete's younger cousins while Mary went to the store. But, otherwise, we were rarely admitted to the room.

Sitting in the front room waiting for the bus, Pete began to get restless. He jumped to his feet and walked to the window, staring out to the south and groaning. "What's taking old Crow Bait so long today?" he asked. That's how Pete referred to our bus driver, an old, retired military man who was overly strict on the bus.

Still anxious, Pete walked to the front door, cracked it open, and stared down the barren blacktop road. The cold wind from the blue northern was howling at about forty miles an hour. Looking past Pete, I noticed that it had started to blow snowflakes across the yard. Pete pulled his head back inside and turned to me.

"Let's tell Mary it's snowing and we can't go to school," he said. Pete generally called his mother by her first name when speaking to others, but he called her "Momma" when speaking directly to her. "All we gotta do is somehow miss the bus. I know old Crow Bait will run off and leave us here if we're not out at the road by the time he gets here. And with it snowing, Mary won't take us to school. She hates driving on snow and ice."

As usual, we devised a brilliant plan. Pete would go out to the gravel driveway that led to the blacktop road, and, when the bus got close, he would wave it on using a dishtowel. We had seen Mary do this before at times when Red would be going into town and Pete and I were allowed to ride along rather than take the bus. In the meantime, my job was to act sick, as if I were going to throw up, which would keep Mary busy in the bathroom until the bus had passed.

While I was still in the bathroom with Mary, I heard Pete running down the hall. He stuck his head in the bathroom and said, "I think we missed the bus."

"Pete, you're not pulling that on me," replied Mary. "Get your butt back out there and watch for that bus." Then, she immediately turned to me with a look that said, "You're probably involved in this too."

Feeling found out, I mumbled, "I think I feel better."

"You get back out there too," prodded Mary.

"Yes, Ma'am," I answered, returning to the front room to find Pete slouched in a big stiff-backed chair looking disappointed.

"Did the bus really go by?" I asked.

"No," sighed Pete with a frown. The bus hadn't come, leaving Pete with no chance to wave it on while Mary had been busy with me in the bathroom.

Pete slowly got out of the big chair and dragged his feet over to the front door. "I'm gonna walk out to the road and see if I can see the bus."

"OK," I answered as Pete put on his coat and walked out the door.

I was sitting on the couch along the west wall of the front room. I was about half asleep and didn't notice how long Pete had been outside. Suddenly, I heard the springs on the screen door begin to squeak as someone pulled open the door. I saw Pete's head peeking around the door. But his frown had turned to a huge grin and he had that familiar glint in his eyes. Pete had another idea!

Pete excitedly stepped into the front room and quickly shut the door behind him. He was puffing out long breaths of air as if he had been running.

"Quick! Come here and look what I found!"

I ran over to the door. As soon as I looked out onto the porch, I saw what he meant. There, standing on the porch, frozen by the cold wind into a perfectly solid upright position, was a skunk.

"Ain't that cool!" Pete exclaimed.

Staring wide-eyed at the skunk, I could immediately imagine innumerable reasons why Pete and I shouldn't have to go to school that day. Pete relayed the story of how he had found the skunk out beside the blacktop road by the mailbox. We both assumed that it had been hit by a car and killed. The amazing thing was that it had no odor whatsoever and was frozen into a perfect standing position, just as if it had frozen standing up.

Pete and I quickly talked over possible scenarios of what we might do with the skunk. The first thing that occurred to us, and the simplest, was to scare Pete's mother, Mary. We made our plan and put it into action.

Pete nonchalantly strolled to the back porch where some farm tools and other equipment was stored. There, he cut a piece of fishing line from one of the fishing rods and brought it back to the front room.

We used two pieces of fishing line. We tied one end of the first line to the skunk's tail and the other end to a brick, which we hung off the side of the porch. The weight of the brick would drag the skunk backward. The second line, we tied around the skunk's neck so that we could drag it forward. When we had finished, the skunk moved both forward and backward. We could pull the skunk forward using the line, or we could let some slack into the line and the skunk would be dragged backward by the weight of the brick.

Now, if you recall, Pete was legally blind without his glasses. And his entire family, on both sides, had major hereditary problems with their eyesight. This handicap, we figured, would work perfectly in our favor.

As we set up the skunk on the porch, we were already laughing at what we thought would be Mary's reaction. Once set, we lay down on the floor at the north end of the couch where I had been sitting earlier. We gave the line a few tugs and saw that it honestly looked as if the skunk were jumping over the door ledge to get into the house. We were already so tickled that we thought Mary might hear us and our fun would be ruined before we even got the chance to perform our stunt.

Finally, Pete whispered, "Stay down behind the couch and I'll go get Mary." I think he enjoyed being the one who would warn the family of impending danger. He walked down the hallway and into the kitchen.

"Momma! Hurry! Come quick! There's a skunk trying to get into the house!"

"Whaaaaat?!" I heard Mary exclaim.

Pete came running back down the hall and into the front room where he jumped down behind the couch where I was hiding. A few seconds later the fun started.

Reaching the doorway from the hall to the front room, Mary let out a high-pitched shriek. "Oh, my! Pete, don't let that thing get into the house!" Suddenly, we began to see objects flying at the skunk from where Mary was standing in the arched doorway. There were rolled-up newspapers, a couple of farm magazines that had been laying on a side table by the phone, and two terry cloth house slippers.

Every time Mary tossed something at the skunk I would simply let some slack into the line and the weight of the brick would pull the skunk back out onto the porch. We soon noticed that the further we pulled the skunk toward the doorway, the higher Mary's screams became, and the further she would retreat into the hallway.

Pete and I were both doubled up on the floor consumed with laughter. This was turning out to be even funnier than we had imagined. Pete was lying flat on his back. He had been giggling so hard that he couldn't sit up straight. Once he managed to get off the floor, he whispered, "I wonder what she would do if we pulled it all the way into the house?" Grabbing the fishing line away from me, he gave it a swift, hard yank.

The skunk looked as if it had suddenly jumped into the living room. We heard Mary scream her highest pitch yet. She then turned and ran down the hall toward the other end of the house.

With Mary gone, Pete and I were free to roll on the floor with laughter. And we did just that until about thirty seconds later, when I saw six inches of the barrel of a twelve-gauge shotgun sticking out of the archway door to the hall. The next thing I saw was a huge ball of fire which extended about three feet from the end of the barrel. (This was before smokeless powder).

Pete had been lying on his back when the shot was fired. In a split second he was on his feet, peering through a cloud of blue smoke at a sight which caused him to shout at the top of his lungs, "Red's gonna kill us all!"

We all three stood staring at a four-inch wide, two-foot long gash in the new white carpet just inside the front door. Mary's shot had blown the skunk into two or three frozen pieces and had scattered about fourteen million tiny shards of nylon fabric through the air. They floated around like snowflakes.

Pete and I looked at Mary, who was not very happy and still holding the shotgun. We were jabbering as fast as we could trying to explain what had just happened, when we heard the door open on the back porch and footsteps coming down the hall toward the living room.

I immediately started down the hall toward the back door, followed closely by Pete. As we met Red coming down the hall, he stuck his arm across the hallway to block our escape.

"What was all that yelling and screaming about? Was that a gunshot?"

"Yeah!" replied Pete. "Mary shot a skunk!"

"What do you mean, she shot a skunk?" Red let us go and headed on to the front room. Pete and I continued to the back door, now at a full run.

We hadn't quite made it out of the house when we heard Red yell, "Those two…!"

As I ran from the house I tried to determine what range Red could effectively hit me with bird shot. From the hole in the carpet, I knew quite well what might happen at a range of twelve feet.

Needless to say, Pete and I didn't catch the bus that day.

❧The Preacher's Poultice❧

It was late August. The temperatures were averaging about a hundred and five degrees outside. Most people tried to spend their afternoons indoors by the fan. But Pete and I either fished or gathered bait so that we could fish in the evenings after milking. This time of year it was hard to find bait because all the crawfish ponds had dried up from the heat.

We had just come home from the sand hills behind the hay barn on the west side of the house. In these hills behind the barn, Pete and I caught grasshoppers and sand crickets for fish bait.

As we entered the house, we could hear Mary talking on the phone to someone about the preacher. It seemed that while he had been working with a young colt, he had gotten tangled in a lariat rope and twisted his knee and thigh muscles so badly that he couldn't walk, leaving him confined to bed.

Now, what this meant for Pete and me was that without a preacher to preach, there would be no church. For two teenage boys like us, that was good news. No church to take up Sunday morning meant more fishing for Pete and me.

Of course, we didn't mention these feelings to Mary when she told us of Brother Paul's unfortunate accident. Instead, Pete commented that he would be remembering Brother Paul in his prayers that night. But I knew that he was simply sucking up to Mary so that we could use the pickup on Sunday to go fishing. It was Mary who usually gave us permission to use the truck to go to the river, because Red was often off on the tractor somewhere in one of the fields and would stay out until milking time.

Later, Pete and I had settled down at the kitchen table and were enjoying cold glasses of iced tea when Mary walked into the room. While scurrying around the kitchen, she said, "I want you two boys to take the pickup and go up to Margaret and Pearl's house and pick up a poultice they've made for Brother Paul's knee."

Back then, country folk had handed down, from one generation to the next, more old wives' tale remedies than one could imagine. Pete and I avoided my grandmother's house for precisely this reason. To my grandmother, if you weren't obese you were "wormy." Her eyesight was bad, and if you got within ten feet of her she'd say, "Come here, boy! You look wormy!" She would then make you eat a teaspoon full of sugar that was soaked with turpentine. It wasn't pleasant.

Some of the other folk remedies that I can recall included skunk fat on a cloth wrapped around one's neck for bronchitis, chewing on some kind of root for upset stomach, and many other "remedies" which would be considered malpractice by most tribal witch doctors.

At any rate, Mary ordered Pete and me to go and fetch the poultice from Margaret and Pearl and take it to Brother Paul's wife. We didn't really mind taking the poultice to Brother Paul. It just meant that we could take our time and cruise the old truck around the sand hills for an hour or so.

When we arrived at the twins' house, I jumped out of the truck and ran up to the door and knocked. Miss Pearl came to the front door and I informed her that Mary had sent us to pick up the poultice for Brother Paul. Miss Pearl told me to go out to the truck and get Pete so that she could give us instructions on how to use the poultice for Brother Paul.

Out at the truck, Pete said, "I ain't smearing that stuff on him. His old lady can do that."

I assured Pete that Miss Pearl had no intention of us administering the remedy, and that she probably just wanted some company. Anyway, she needed to make sure we got the directions right so we could properly relay them to the preacher's wife.

When we got in the house, Miss Pearl notified us that Miss Margaret was out in the blackberry patch, and began telling us about everything the two of them had put into the poultice and for what reason. Pete and I stood there like first-year medical students, nodding our heads and saying, "Yes, ma'am." It wasn't vital that we get all of the information. We knew that as soon as we left her house, Pearl would be on the phone with Mary giving her the same directions so that she could keep us straight. Nonetheless, Pete and I stood quietly and listened to the whole story.

At length, Pearl finished her lesson and went behind some white cotton curtains that covered a pantry in the kitchen. She emerged with a half-gallon jar of what looked like green salsa. There seemed to be a number of different plants and leaves that had been chopped up into deep green mulch and placed inside the jar. I reached out and took it from Miss Pearl as Pete got the last few details of instruction. We then went back out to the truck and started down the sandy road toward the preacher's house.

I noticed as I drove that Pete would stare intently at the jar, and then would glance out toward the roadside. Suddenly he burst out laughing. This was the sign that he had been "thinking" again.

"Hey, you know what would be funny?" he began.

"What?"

"Pull over down here and I'll show you."

Just down the road Pete indicated a spot to stop, and jumped out of the truck. As I walked around to where he stood, I noticed that he was staring at a huge poison ivy vine growing all the way to the top of a twelve-foot blackjack tree. The vine was so large that it had covered almost the entire tree. I looked on in astonishment as Pete dumped about half of the poultice out onto the ground and gave me a big, toothy, evil smile.

There was no need to reveal his plan as he started to grab handfuls of poison ivy leaves, tear them into small pieces and place them in the jar with the rest of the poultice. At first, I was apprehensive. But then I remembered the preacher's remark to Red one day that, "Those two boys have an itch and don't know where to scratch it." I figured it was only fair to give the preacher an itch that he couldn't scratch either.

As we filled the jar with ivy leaves, we once again began to laugh at the thought of what would happen. When the jar was completely full, we stirred the concoction with a stick to make sure it was blended well. Then, immediately, we drove to the next mile section of county road where there was a metal water trough and washed our hands repeatedly, buffing them with sand between washings to make sure that they were perfectly clean and free of poison.

Once we arrived at Brother Paul's house, we carried the nasty concoction into the house to Brother Paul's wife and Pete relayed the instructions we were given from Miss Pearl.

"She said to apply the poultice all over Brother Paul's knee and thigh. Rub it in really well, all the way up to the inside of his…uh…crotch. After you rub it in, cover it with a warm towel. It will pull out all of the soreness in the muscle."

Finally, somehow without even cracking a smile, Pete added, "Miss Pearl said not to take it off if it starts to itch because that will be the point when it is working its best."

On the drive home, Pete and I were in tears with laughter. We had just pulled off the perfect crime. And it would be the old twins, not us, who would get the blame for a botched poultice.

We had been home about four hours when we heard a tap at the door. Pete opened it to find the preacher's wife. Visibly flustered, she asked if Mary were home.

"Sure," replied Pete. "Come on in." He pushed the door open for her to enter.

Finding Mary, the preacher's wife began to tell her how she had just come from the twins' house, but they weren't home. She meant to learn about the ingredients in the poultice that they had made. She appeared truly desperate as she began to tell Mary how Brother Paul was reacting to the poultice. He had broken out into whelps. His eyes, lips and groin were all swelling and he was having trouble breathing. It was evident that he was having a severe allergic reaction to the something in the poultice.

"Paul is extremely allergic to poison oak and poison ivy. He's been hospitalized twice for it in the past," she continued.

It was about this point that Red walked into the room. With great concern, the women relayed to him the whole story of the poultice and Brother Paul's reaction to it.

Pete and I were now, of course, racked with fear. We might have meant to pull a trick on the preacher, but we certainly didn't want to kill him. Finally, Pete broke our silence, "You'd better take him to the hospital. That poultice has probably got poison ivy in it."

The muscles in Red's face tightened as he clenched his teeth and turned to Pete. "Margaret and Pearl know what poison ivy looks like, Pete," he growled. "How do you reckon poison ivy could have gotten into that poultice?"

The veins were popping out in Red's forehead. "You better start talking, boy. And I mean now," he said through his teeth.

Compliantly, Pete began to confess his sins and explain how innocent his intentions had been when he placed the poison ivy in the jar, as if it mattered. As Pete spilled his guts, I was slowly shuffling away from Red and looking toward the back door. It was about this point that Pete stopped using "I" and started using "we."

In all the times our plans had gone awry, this is the first time I can recall Red not erupting into a verbal rage. I attribute this single respite to the fact that the preacher's wife was present.

"Mary and I are going to take Paul and his wife to the hospital," Red said as calmly as he could muster. "I'll deal with you boys when we get back." I couldn't believe his display of emotional discipline. Nor could I believe that he would give Pete and me two hours head start before he came back to kill us.

As Red, Mary, and the preacher's wife headed toward the door, I could still hear the sound of Red's teeth grinding.

⊱How to Stop the Preacher⊰

Pete and I were outside lying in the shade with our backs against the cement cellar one day when the preacher, Brother Paul, pulled into the yard.

"I wonder what he wants this time," groaned Pete.

We had noticed that when the preacher showed up it wasn't usually just for a friendly visit or to pray for wayward souls. It usually involved manual labor for Pete and me. It would usually be Mary who would ask us to please go and help Brother Paul, knowing that we would give in to her pleas. At any rate, Pete made the comment that he wished the preacher would stop coming around.

A few weeks after this, the Estep boys' aunt passed away and left an unusually large dog. The boys were trying to find a home for this dog they called "Rock." Knowing that Rock had a bad attitude toward visitors, especially preachers, Pete decided that he wanted to have the dog.

Pete and I went to talk to Mary. We discussed adopting poor Rock so that he wouldn't have to be put to sleep or possibly shot as a stray. Finally, we convinced her to let us keep the dog and assured her that we would take full responsibility for Rock's care. Actually, Rock turned out to be a very astute guard dog and the arrangement proved good for everyone involved. But how he would respond to the preacher had yet to be tested.

Later that same fall, Pete and I were at my house watching my father get his traps ready for trapping season. He was explaining all the little things someone would need to know to be an expert trapper and to be able to catch bobcats and coyotes professionally.

He had told us that coyotes could be thought of simply as wild dogs because they have many of the same habits that dogs have. He made a point to emphasize that coyotes, like dogs, like to smell everything and everywhere, especially when they can detect that another coyote has been present. Moreover, coyotes mark their territory by urinating on different objects.

My dad was in full lecture mode, talking about how dogs and coyotes mark their turf, when he blurted out, "Here, I'll just show you." He walked to one of his little sheds and returned with a can of truck brake fluid. He explained that brake fluid smells just like urine to a dog or coyote and that he had used it to catch coyotes on occasion. He also explained that this odor was the reason dogs are prone to urinate on truck tires and wheels.

At last, my dad walked over to a fence row that had mule tail weeds growing in it and pulled one of the weeds. Pete and I watched as he dipped the end of the weed into the brake fluid and rubbed it against a small apricot tree that was close by, as well as on a couple of fence posts along the fence row. After he finished, he called for the three old dogs that we had hanging around the house. They had been in the front of the house, probably sleeping. When they arrived at the back, the dogs immediately began smelling everything nearby. Sure enough, they went straight to the apricot tree and both fence posts, hiked their legs, and urinated on the places where my dad had spread the brake fluid.

My dad gave a big laugh. "See, I told you so."

I turned to Pete and saw that he had that look on his face of deep thought. Later, on the way back to his house, he said, "I can't wait until the preacher comes to visit." That was all he ever said. This was one time that Pete never let me in on his plan.

A couple weeks later, Pete and I were sitting in the kitchen when we heard Rock barking wildly outside. Mary walked to the window and peeked out. "It's Brother Paul," she said. "You boys go out and keep Rock off of him so he can get to the house."

Pete jumped up and made a mad dash out the back door. I wondered why he was in such a hurry. As I walked out the back, there stood Pete with a can of brake fluid that he had strategically hidden in the well-house just outside the back door. He also had a long mule tail weed in his hand. He turned to me with a huge smile. "Let's go help the preacher!"

As we approached the preacher's car, Pete yelled at him not to get out yet, because Rock would chew his leg off. Pete made his way to the car, opened the door, and informed the preacher to walk slowly toward the house. As the preacher walked, baby-stepping toward the house, Rock followed him with a deep guttural growl, hair bristling down the middle of his back. Unnoticed by the preacher, Pete was pouring a few drops of the brake fluid on the leaves of the weed in his hand.

Once the preacher made it to the porch, Pete yelled, "Don't touch that door or Rock will take your hand off!"

The preacher stopped and stood shaking as Pete approached him from behind, all the time warning the preacher of the consequences should he make any sudden moves.

As Pete came up behind the preacher, he reached out with the weed and lightly brushed the back of the preacher's pant leg with the brake fluid. Immediately, Rock bounced up onto the porch where the preacher was standing. And just as quickly, Pete reminded him not to move. The preacher stood like a statue as Rock began to sniff the backs of his pant legs, then hiked his leg and soaked both legs of the preacher's pants. When Rock had finished his business, Pete swatted him on the butt with the weed, scolding him for his inexcusable behavior. The dog trotted off and the preacher went inside.

The preacher didn't stay long that day, and it was months before he came to the house again. Pete and I both laughed nightly about this prank.

Later that same year, Pete and I accompanied Red to the livestock sale at Watonga. There were a number of older men hanging along the fence, looking over the rails at the cattle as they were being unloaded. Pete somehow managed to find some brake fluid in the toolbox of the truck and soaked a weed with it. He walked along the fence and brushed as many pant legs as he could without being noticed.

Shortly, a truck load of cattle came in, accompanied by several blue heeler cow dogs. Pete and I sat in the truck and laughed as the cow dogs took turns soaking the pant legs of the old men's overalls.

Twenty years later, Pete still kept a can of brake fluid handy at his house.

༄The Science Lesson༄

Pete and I had just entered the house and come through the back door and down the hallway into the kitchen. Mary and Red were both in the kitchen, which was unusual. Mary was at the stove and Red was sitting at the table. As Pete and I entered with armloads of school books, Red asked his usual question: "Did you learn anything at school today?"

At this point, it was normal for Pete to roll his eyes and give his stock answer: "Of course not." But on this day I beat him to the punch.

"Yeah, man. We learned something really cool," I piped up excitedly. After years of dealing with Red, I knew that he sometimes forgot who he was dealing with and let his guard down. This was one of those days, and he took the bait.

"What did you learn today that was so cool?" he asked.

"Well," I began calmly, "We learned that water can be magnetized." I could see immediately that I had his attention.

"What do you mean you can magnetize water?"

"It's kind of hard to explain," I said, "but to make it simple, you can actually pin a glass of water to the wall, or to anything metal, after it has been magnetized."

I could tell the wheels were turning in Red's mind about what I had said. A few seconds later, he blurted out, "What kind of bull are they teaching you at school? That's impossible."

"No, not really," I retorted. "We saw it done today at school. Mr. England pinned a jar of water to a metal filing cabinet in our class."

Red and I began to argue. Pete had no idea what I was up to, but from being my partner in crime all this time he knew that he needed to take the lead. "Well, I lost a dollar bet today because I thought it couldn't be done either," he bellowed.

The discussion became more heated as Pete and I bantered with Red, feeding him our line of malarkey. We jabbered on about the molecular weight of water versus metal and how the closer the molecules got together, the more easily they were magnetized. We pulled out every word or phrase we had ever heard in science class, trying to convince Red of our scientific prowess. But it was all to no avail, as finally he shouted, "Do you boys think I'm totally stupid? I know that a glass of water can't be pinned to the wall!"

We had Red worked into a frenzy and the doors of opportunity had opened. "I can prove it to you," I said. "I can do it myself."

"I'll bet you can't!" Red snapped back.

"All right," I offered. "If you'll help me, I can prove to you that a glass of water can be pinned to the wall."

Quickly, I started putting together a list of equipment. I asked Mary to get me the biggest metal safety pin she could find. I then turned to Pete and asked him to go to the junk drawer and retrieve two small, round magnets that he and I had taken out of a transistor radio earlier in the summer. I went out to the shed and picked up a wide-mouthed quart mason jar off of the shelf. I also gathered a handful of rusty metal particles from the inside of an old coffee can. Finally, I returned to the kitchen to Red, who was still sitting at the table.

Mary came in with a large metal safety pin, about two inches long, which had once been a diaper pin. I congratulated her and commented that the type of metal in the pin would only make my experiment work better. The experiment had everyone's attention, even Pete, who still didn't know what I was doing.

I asked Mary to fill the jar with ice water as cold as she could make it. I explained that the colder the water, the closer the water particles would gather, and, therefore, the more easily they could be magnetized. Once it was filled with ice cold water, she set it on the table.

I took the two magnets, the safety pin, and the rusty dust and began to prepare the experiment, all the time commenting on how wonderfully things were coming along. "This is going to be great!" I exclaimed. "It's going to work just like it did today at school!" I used the magnets to magnetize the pin and pick up the rust particles, giving some credibility to the idea that the water would also be magnetized.

"OK, Pete," I said, "When I tell you, I want you to drop both magnets into the water. Make sure they are stuck together and slid all the way to the side of the jar." I explained that he should then stand back to give me room to maneuver. I told my audience that I would then place the safety pin on the outside of the glass, next to the magnets on the inside, and use it to pin the jar to the metal object of our choosing, which was the refrigerator in the corner.

"Now, Red," I said, "get over here if you want to see this. Water, unlike metal, will only stay magnetized for a very short time."

Mary's curiosity was piqued. She walked closer and stared at the jar as if she fully expected it to stick to the side of the refrigerator. Finally, Red drew his chair up, clearly expecting a miracle. I practiced putting the safety pin firmly against the side of the jar and pressing the jar to the refrigerator. I encouraged Red to move still closer.

Finally, I asked Pete if he was ready. "It's a go!" he shouted.

"OK," I said. "Here we go! Pete, drop the magnets!" I saw the two magnets drop into the jar and slide perfectly to one side. Then, I pressed the safety pin to the side of the jar next to the magnets and acted as if I were going to press the jar against the refrigerator. Instead, I purposely dropped the pin.

"I dropped the pin!" I yelled. "Red, pick it up or the experiment won't work right!"

Red lunged forward in his chair, head between his knees to pick up the safety pin. As he did, I dumped the full quart of freezing ice water on his head and down his back. Then, I ran.

It was hard to get traction on the wet linoleum floor, but I ended up with a good lead on him going out the back door.

"Why, you…!" I heard him yelling.

I knew the joke had gone well when I also heard Mary cackling at the top of her lungs. Detecting that Pete was not screaming or crying, I determined that I had received full blame for this one.

About a month later, Glen, Pete's older brother, returned home from college at Oklahoma State University for a weekend visit. Pete and I had just entered the kitchen when we heard Red remark to Glen, "Boy, don't they teach you nothin' at college? Even I can pin a jar of water to the wall!"

❧The Wrestler☙

Wrestling is a sport that has a long heritage in Oklahoma, and the little town of Geary has a special place in that history. Today, Geary is still home to one of the oldest and most prestigious high school wrestling tournaments in the state. Pete's older brother, Glen, had been a state champion wrestler in high school and had gone on to wrestle for the storied program at Oklahoma State University. In 1963, Glen took second place at the Big Eight Conference tournament and went on to wrestle in the NCAA national championships. Glen's accomplishments were a source of great pride to the whole town, but especially to Red.

Glen came home from school in the summer of 1963 with the goal of winning a national championship the following year. He had it in his mind to improve his stamina over the summer. Often, while Pete and I were milking or doing other chores, Glen would take off running. He had a habit of running around the section of land that we lived on. Each section line road was one mile. In all, it would be four miles around the section. But it was tough running. The roads were not paved, but instead were covered with nasty, wind-blown sand that could be fairly deep in some places.

Red never bothered Glen with chores. He talked all over town about how good a wrestler Glen was and how he had been runner-up in the Big Eight. He just let Glen do his running. At that point, Geary seemed poised to have its first national wrestling champion and Red was already getting his bragging speech ready for the domino hall.

Pete was never jealous of Glen as you might imagine. On the contrary, he was as proud of his brother as anyone. One day, Pete saw Glen jog out of the driveway to run the section line roads. Unknown to the rest of us, Pete decided that he would hop in the car and follow Glen while he ran. Whether Glen knew Pete was following him or not, I don't know.

Now, Glen had a certain method of training. He would jog for a while, then break loose into an all-out sprint until he couldn't run any longer, and then return to a jog. Pete knew this and slowly trailed Glen in the car as Glen jogged along. When Pete saw Glen burst into his run, he suddenly got curious about how fast Glen was running. So, he took off in the car, accelerating along behind Glen and watching the speedometer as he drove. Later, Pete recalled to us that he had been muttering to himself, "Ten, fifteen...Man, he's really moving!...Twenty! Twenty-five!..."

BLOOP! BLOOP! That was the sound Pete heard as Glen's body tumbled under the car. While he had been paying attention to the speedometer, Pete had forgotten to actually keep an eye on Glen. He had run clean over him. Pete turned around and loaded Glen, who was alive but injured, into the car. In a panic, Pete returned to the house and found us.

"I ran over Glen!" he yelled.

We looked at him in puzzlement, not knowing that he had ever left the house. Of course, there was also the fact that Pete was a habitual liar and Red had been fooled by him all too often. Eventually, however, he convinced Red to look in the car.

Luckily, the deep sand had cushioned Glen and saved him from death or maiming injury. But he was a bloody, sandy mess. And his back was hurt. We took him to the hospital where he recovered well enough.

As for his wrestling career, Glen never won a national championship. In fact, he never so much as placed in the Big Eight again. I guess no one will ever know exactly why, but silently, we all blamed Pete.

❧The Watermelon❧

It was August. Pete and I were in our mid-teens and had gotten used to hard work. We had done everything from helping build barns to hauling hay. And I mean a lot of hay. My dad, Charley, had hay trucks, and when we weren't milking for Red, we were hauling square bales of alfalfa hay for my dad. I think Red and my dad both liked to see us sweat, or maybe they just wanted to keep us tired so that we would stay out of trouble. In any case, the alfalfa hay was put up for the winter to feed the milk cows when the pastures were dead or covered with snow. Feeding alfalfa also helped keep the feed bill down on the amount of ground feed that we used.

One day at Pete's house, we had finished our chores and were getting ready to head toward the hay fields. Red walked out of the milk barn to where Pete and I were filling the water cooler from the well by the cattle corral.

"You boys won't be hauling hay today," he announced. "I called Charley and told him I needed you two to run over to Mr. Snodgrass's and pick up a load of rye seed. I'm going to drill pasture up on the sand hills west of the barn."

On sandy ground like the sand hills, most people planted rye for pasture instead of wheat. Sometimes it was even broadcast by airplane because the ground was too soft for a tractor.

Going to get the rye seed sounded like a great idea to Pete and me. We would have done just about anything to get out of hauling hay.

"Sure, we'll run over and get you some rye," we said, jumping at the opportunity.

At the time we didn't know exactly how much rye seed we were supposed to be picking up, but it didn't matter. We were just concerned about staying out of the hay fields.

While we finished filling our water jug, Red walked to the top of the hill and got the wheat truck with side boards. Pete and I knew then that this was a special occasion, as we had never been turned loose with the big truck before.

"You boys go over to Mr. Snodgrass's farm," said Red. "He'll show you where the rye bin is. I want you to get three hundred bushels of rye, bring it back, and put it in the granary up by the barn on the hill."

At that age, Pete and I had no idea how much three hundred bushels was, but it couldn't be all that bad. The two of us loaded up in the truck and took off for the Snodgrass farm. Mr. Snodgrass lived about ten miles northwest of Calumet and about three miles straight east of the Estep boys' house. On our way, we discussed what we would do when we finished with the rye seed project. Fishing and swimming were always at the top of our list, so this was what we talked about as we drove.

About three miles north of the Snodgrass farm was a small, but very deep, gypsum pond. The Moore boys, who lived close by, had built a wooden diving board on the edge of the pond and all the local farm boys swam there. In the end, we decided that we would drop by the Moore pond for an afternoon swim on the way home with the truckload of rye.

Mr. Snodgrass came out to meet us when we arrived at his house. Standing in his fenced front yard, he told us that Red had already discussed with him that we were to load three hundred bushels of rye seed. He also said that Red had mentioned that he should keep a close eye on us, but we assured Mr. Snodgrass that Red's concern about our behavior was based on hearsay and that Pete and I were utterly harmless, hardworking farm hands.

Escorting us out to his barn, Mr. Snodgrass showed us where the rye was located in a wooden bin in the hallway of the old barn. Right away Pete and I recognized that the hallway was too narrow to back the truck down to where the rye bin was. After a short discussion with Mr. Snodgrass, he suggested that we take five gallon buckets and scoop the rye from the bin into the buckets, then carry them to the back of the truck.

Now, we figured that a five gallon bucket full of rye weighs about fifty pounds. It is also substantially less than a bushel. Quickly working out the math, we determined that we would each have to make several hundred trips down the hallway carrying fifty pound buckets, which we would then have to lift head-high over the sideboards of the truck to dump. Suddenly, hay hauling didn't sound so bad after all. At least while hauling hay we would rest between loads.

As we stood assessing our situation, Mr. Snodgrass commented, "Now, you boys stay out here by the barn because Momma's got a big ol' black Rottweiler dog. She calls him 'Compact', and he bites. She named him Compact because he can crush an armadillo with just one bite."

I suddenly remembered seeing a sign inside the fence in the front yard that said BEWARE OF…but the rest of the sign was unreadable because the bottom had been chewed off.

Mr. Snodgrass went back to the house and Pete and I went to work loading rye. We hauled buckets of rye for about an hour. Then Pete jumped up to look into the bed of the truck to see how much we had loaded.

"This job stinks!" he said in his usual cynical tone. Red had always said that Pete was a pessimist and that even his blood type was "B-Negative."

We would have been better off had we gone to the hayfield. I remembered Mr. Snodgrass saying that our truck could probably hold about four hundred bushels. That meant we had to fill the truck three-quarters full. So far, our hour of work had deposited about a hundred bushels in the truck. We got a drink of cool water and went back to hauling buckets up and down the hallway of the barn.

After about another hour or so, Pete said, "I'm hungry."

I reminded him that we couldn't quit until we had the truck loaded. After that we could go home and have Mary fix us some dinner. We went on hauling buckets for a third hour. I was coming down the hallway with a bucket of rye when I saw Mr. Snodgrass approaching us from the corral gate.

"You boys should about have a load," he remarked, climbing up on the side of the truck and looking into the bed.

"Ya'll put about ten more buckets each on the truck. I'll be back in just a minute." He disappeared through the corral gates again.

As Pete and I loaded our last two buckets of rye, I saw Mr. Snodgrass re-emerge from the corral gate. This time he had a large butcher knife in one hand, and three forks in the other.

"You boys follow me," he said.

Without question, we followed him through the corral gate. He led us out to the back of his house where there stood a large windmill. Below the windmill was a big, round cement water tank. Standing beside the water tank, Mr. Snodgrass congratulated us on the hard work we had done.

"You boys sure worked up a hard sweat loading that rye. I thought I'd give you a little reward."

Peering into the water tank, I could see a huge black diamond watermelon floating in the cool water.

"I put this melon in here last night, so it ought to be nice and cold. See if one of you can lift it out here and set it on the ground."

Pete didn't need any prodding. He quickly dove into the tank, retrieved the watermelon, and set it on the ground at Mr. Snodgrass's feet. Then, like an accomplished surgeon, Mr. Snodgrass sliced open the watermelon into two identical pieces using the butcher knife. Handing Pete and me each a fork, he said, "Dig in!"

We didn't hesitate. Within seconds, both our mouths were full of sweet, red, juicy watermelon. While we ate, Mr. Snodgrass began telling us about his watermelon patch. Evidently, he had won numerous awards and prizes for some of the melons he had raised. He even mentioned that he had won a couple of first place awards at the State Fair in Oklahoma City.

But stories about winning prizes were not important to Pete and me at the moment. The only melon we cared about was the one sitting in front of us. We simply kept filling our mouths and nodding politely as Mr. Snodgrass spoke. When we finally couldn't eat any more, I looked over at Pete. He had watermelon juice all over his face and chest. I did too, no doubt. I felt like flopping over on my back for a nice, long nap. To this day I cannot recall enjoying a watermelon more.

Pete and I were too stuffed to move and Mr. Snodgrass seemed to notice.

"You boys rest a bit," he said, washing the butcher knife and forks in the water tank, "then I've got something I want to show you."

We lay there a few minutes, and then finally managed to get to our feet.

"Follow me," Mr. Snodgrass said, starting to walk past the windmill and through a small row of trees that had been planted as a windbreak.

When we emerged on the other side of the trees, we found ourselves standing at the edge of a big watermelon patch. I could see the tops of watermelons rising above the leaves of the plants in at least a hundred places. And every melon was big and dark green.

Mr. Snodgrass led us out into the watermelon patch to a monstrous lump that he had covered in burlap sacks. He pulled back the sacks to reveal an enormous watermelon.

"This beautiful lady is going to win me the blue ribbon at the State Fair next month," he said, beaming. He rubbed his hands all over the melon as if he had some kind of emotional attachment to it.

As he jabbered on about the melon, he always kept referring to it as if it were a woman.

"I keep the burlap sacks wet and put them on her so that she won't get sunburned," he said.

I turned to Pete. Immediately, I could tell that there was envy in his eyes and evil in his heart. I thought about the Ten Commandments' prohibition against coveting thy neighbor's wife, or his manservant, or his ox. I couldn't remember anything about watermelons, though. At any rate, I knew Pete well enough to know that meant to steal the watermelon.

"How does he think we would be able to carry that thing?" I wondered to myself, gazing at the melon, which had to weigh at least a hundred pounds. But, remembering the buckets of rye that we had just hauled weighed about fifty pounds each, I thought we might be able to do it.

Neither Pete nor I commented on Mr. Snodgrass's watermelon patch at the time. Not wanting to give ourselves away, we just kept quiet and listened. Then we loaded back into the truck full of rye seed to head back home.

"You boys come back anytime!" Mr. Snodgrass said as the truck started to roll out of the drive.

Pete, in a low voice from the side of his mouth, replied, "We will." Then, he chuckled to himself in a deep, sinister laugh.

We had barely made it out of the driveway when Pete said, "We need to stop at the Estep boys' house and tell them what we found."

Now, up to this point, I had tried to maintain my innocence.

"What do you mean?" I asked sheepishly.

"You know what I mean!" Pete snarled. "Old Man Snodgrass's watermelon!"

Ah, yes. That big, smooth beauty lying naked in the sun. She was irresistible. I would not be satisfied until I held her in my arms. There was a primal urge welling up from deep inside me, and I knew I had to steal the watermelon.

I looked at Pete, and we both said simultaneously, "We have to have that watermelon!"

We stopped by the Estep boys' house. The boys weren't home, but their dad, Otis, was. We told him that we had been at Mr. Snodgrass's farm loading rye. He climbed up on the sideboards to look at our load.

"Ted and Dale are over at their uncle's house and won't be home until dark," Otis said.

Pete and I continued home with the truck full of rye. But the encounter with the watermelon had drastically altered our plans. Swimming was out; watermelon procurement was in.

We drove up to the granary on the hill and began to unload the rye, bucket by bucket. But there was no thought in our heads except "Big Bertha," as we had dubbed the prize melon. Our work unloading was easier than the loading because we were able to unload directly from the truck into the granary, and, after about two hours, we finished the job.

It was mid-afternoon, and we had eaten only a small lunch because we had still been full from our watermelon feast. We lay against the cement cellar outside to take a nap while we had the chance. We knew Red would be home any time with some type of work for us to do.

While lying there in the shade, we couldn't help but talk about Big Bertha. Pete suggested that we get the Estep boys to help us steal some watermelons. We were finalizing our plans when we heard Red drive into the driveway. We stood up and met him halfway across the yard, immediately letting him know how much work it had been to load the rye.

"Hard work is good for you," he replied. "It makes you want to get an education. I'm going back over to Mr. Snodgrass's house to pay him for the rye. Do you boys want to ride along?"

Without bothering to answer, we took off running to the pickup truck.

At the Snodgrass farm, we jumped out of the pickup and Mr. Snodgrass came out to meet us. He and Red struck up a conversation while Pete and I inconspicuously wandered off in the direction of the watermelon patch. Once out of sight, we broke into a dead run out to where Big Bertha lay. Pete was the first to arrive, and he slowly began to remove the burlap sacks.

"Ain't she a beauty?" he said once the sacks were all off. He was rubbing his hands all over the smooth, green skin of the melon. Finally, he gave it a hug and snuggled down close to it.

"Get up, you idiot!" I said. "Red's probably ready to go."

As Pete reluctantly climbed to his feet, I cased the scene to see what our best approach would be. I noticed something that we had missed before. All along the edge of Mr. Snodgrass's field ran a line of white baling twine. It had been staked down about every twenty feet with small metal posts. Between each post was a soda can that had been filled with marbles. If anything hit the fence, the cans would rattle and alert Mr. Snodgrass.

Pete and I smiled at each other as we shook the fence and rattled one of the cans. This meager defense system would be no match for our epic criminal minds. The heist was on!

Later that evening after milking, we started begging Red to let us use the pickup so that we could go over to the Estep boys' house and play cards. It was not uncommon for us boys to all get together at night and play pitch after we had finished our work. With Mary's prodding, Red finally gave in and said we could use the truck.

It was dusk when we arrived at Ted and Dale's house. We immediately relayed the story about the watermelon patch and our intention to make a raid.

As usual, Ted responded, "We're in." He was the older of the two and spoke for both of them. Dale always followed his lead.

When we told the Esteps about the watermelon patch, we conveniently forgot to mention Big Bertha. She would be ours alone.

According to our plan, Ted would be the driver and would take us to within a quarter mile of the patch. Pete, Dale, and I would then sneak across a grass pasture and into the melon field. As we drove, Ted, who was five years older than us, filled our heads with nonsense stories of people getting shot while stealing watermelons.

"Now, I want you to know," warned Ted, "that nobody gets a ride back to the house unless they bring a watermelon back with them."

We all agreed and made our pact that no one would leave the field without a melon. We also got permission from Ted that Pete and I could bring only one melon between the two of us, as long as it was a big one.

Making our final approach to the field, Pete and I described the landscape to Dale and warned him about the twine fence that Mr. Snodgrass had erected. And, after re-pledging our sacred oath that each person would bring back a watermelon, we got out of the truck and began to make our way through the night into the pasture.

When we finally reached the twine fence, we tried to get our bearings. Everything looked different in the dark, and Pete and I argued over where we thought Big Bertha was located. Ultimately, we agreed on a direction and crawled under the twine fence and out into the watermelon patch.

Every ten seconds or so, I would hear Dale or Pete whisper, "Oooh, there's a big one!"

But I kept reminding Pete that we could not settle for just any big melon. We wanted Big Bertha.

Dale was crawling in the lead and Pete and I were slightly behind and off to one side. Suddenly, Dale dropped to his belly. "Listen, I hear something," he said.

We all stopped crawling and stared out into the darkness, listening as intently as we could. After a few seconds, I assured Dale that he was just nervous and jittery and that he was hearing things. He started to crawl again, but stopped almost immediately. Pete and I eased up beside him.

"It sounds like something growling," he said.

I started to laugh at his hallucinations, but then I heard a sound as well. Suddenly, the silence of the night was broken by the sound of a snarling, snapping Rottweiler dog that was headed directly for us.

It was at this moment that I learned the perils of trying to run through a watermelon patch in the dark. I was up and down ten times in the first twenty feet.

Mr. Snodgrass had staked his dog, Compact, in the watermelon patch, right next to Big Bertha. I heard the chain rattling as he charged out toward where Pete, Dale, and I were. A few seconds later, I heard someone, either Pete or Dale, hit the twine fence. The sound of cans and marbles rattling out through the pasture filled the night air.

Then I heard the sound of a man's voice shouting, "I'm gonna shoot you boys!"

BOOM! BOOM! I heard the hair-raising sound of pellets zipping through the air above my head.

I made it to the pasture, but I was wounded. I had twisted my ankle running through the watermelons and had almost broken my left wrist on a fall. I managed to make it to the road where Ted had dumped us out. But Ted was not there.

I started to walk down the sandy road toward home. I was concerned about Pete and Dale. After all, they had been closer to the dog than I had been when the action started. I wondered if I hadn't heard the sound of bones being crushed.

After a few minutes of walking, I heard a vehicle coming toward me and recognized the sound of the old pickup truck. I stood and waited until Ted drove up beside me. Pete was already in the truck.

"Where's Dale?" he asked.

I told him I didn't know, adding that it was possible that he had been eaten by Compact or shot by Mr. Snodgrass.

"I can't go home and tell Momma that Dale got shot stealing watermelons," said Ted, almost in tears.

"Maybe he's down the road somewhere," I suggested.

"Let's go look."

We drove the whole mile of the section line road. When there was still no sign of Dale, we all became worried. We wondered whether he had been captured by Mr. Snodgrass. Ted stopped the truck again, and we stood on the dark road in front of it.

Suddenly, we heard the sound of footsteps running toward us. Ted jumped into the truck and turned on the headlights. There was Dale, running down the middle of the road carrying a tiny watermelon about the size of a grapefruit.

He ran up to where we were standing, handed the melon to Ted, and jumped into the back of the truck.

"I ain't walking home," he said.

Turns out Dale had not managed to get a watermelon on our initial trip into the patch and had gone back and grabbed the first melon he could find so that we wouldn't make him walk home. We laughed all the way back home about the fun we'd had, even though our plan was a complete failure and Big Bertha still lay in the patch safe from our lusts.

The next day I could barely get out of bed. Red questioned us about how it could be possible to twist an ankle and almost break a wrist by playing cards. Luckily, he seemed to miss the rope burns Pete had from getting caught up in the twine.

As I got older and reflected on this story, a thought came to my mind. I wondered if Red hadn't set the whole thing up, scheming with Mr. Snodgrass and knowing that Pete and I couldn't resist stealing that watermelon once we knew it was there. I guess I'll never know for certain.

≫Red's Fish≪

During the early part of spring, Pete and I would fish for largemouth bass in some of the local farm ponds. Among our favorite spots were the clear water ponds in the gypsum canyons north of Pete's house. In most of these ponds, the timber had been left standing when they had been dammed, making the ponds great hangouts for black bass. Many of these ponds were large compared to their muddy stock pond counterparts. The stock ponds were great for catching waterdogs and crawfish for bait, but the canyon ponds were better for bass fishing.

The gypsum ponds were northeast of the house toward Okarche. Quite a few were well over five acres in surface area, which I guess technically made them small lakes. Besides black bass, the ponds also held channel catfish. Some of the locals we knew had caught catfish that might have broken the state record, had they been weighed and certified. We knew of plenty of fish that would have weighed more than twenty pounds.

It had become a regular thing for Pete and me to go with some of our friends on overnight camping trips to one of these lakes and fish for catfish all night long. Occasionally, we would be accompanied by one of the other boys' fathers or older brothers. Once in a while, Red would even go with us.

Pete and I were standing in the milk barn talking about some of the fish stories that had been circulating recently in the community. There was a lot of talk about the big catfish that were being caught in the local ponds.

Now, every family seemed to have its own particular secret fishing hole. But the names of the pond owners or the locations were never revealed. Pete and I had a secret hole as well. The pond belonged to a man named Alan Stroud who lived north of Calumet and just happened to be friends with both our fathers. Though I'm not certain it had a proper name, Pete and I always referred to it as "Stroud Lake."

Stroud Lake was approximately eight acres in size. It was full of old, downed timber and huge gypsum rock mounds where an old gypsum pit had been located before the canyon had been dammed up. Some of the water around the gypsum pits had to be thirty feet deep or more. All I knew was that Pete and I were both excellent swimmers and neither of us could touch the bottom.

We had caught our share of fish out of the lake that were in the ten- to twelve-pound range. But, like every dreaming fisherman, we had always believed that somewhere in the lake there had to be at least one huge catfish that would break every known record. This was the fish that Pete, Red, and I always fished for when we went to Stroud Lake.

As Pete and I stood telling fish stories, Red turned to us. "If you boys will go gather up some bait we'll go over to Stroud Lake on Friday night and fish for a while." We immediately agreed and started making plans for an all-night fishing trip.

Friday evening after milking, we packed the equipment into the truck. We had a full load of quilts, sleeping bags, fishing poles, lanterns, folding chairs, and buckets full of bait.

Pete and I had also invited the Estep boys, Ted and Dale, to come with us. It was common practice to blindfold anyone that went with us so that they couldn't reveal our secret spot, only to hear them say upon arrival, "Oh, I've been here before!" Anyway, by the time we picked up Ted and Dale and made it to the lake, it was getting dark.

The first order from Red once we got out of the truck was to gather firewood while he got his poles out. Red always used eight- or ten-foot fiberglass rods with thirty-pound line and huge treble hooks. His philosophy was, "You can't catch a big fish if you don't use big bait."

As we gathered the wood, Red baited out four of his biggest poles and placed them in rod holders in front of his marked fishing spot. This was Red's signal to us boys that we should move away from him and find somewhere else to fish. So, after the fire was built, Ted, Dale, Pete, and I all gathered our stuff and started across the dam to the other side of the lake, leaving Red comfortably in front of the fire watching his poles.

I can't remember a slower night of fishing. It was about two o'clock in the morning and no one had gotten so much as a nibble. Pete and I had run out of topics of conversation with the Esteps and the food that Mary had sent us had long been exhausted. We were ready to quit.

"Go see if Red's ready to go," said Pete, turning to me. "Tell him we haven't caught anything and we're ready to go home and get something to eat."

"OK," I replied, starting back across the dam to where Red was fishing.

As I approached the campfire, I noticed that Red had gotten one of the reclining chairs from out of the truck and was sitting in it close to the fire. Upon closer inspection, I saw that he was in a deep sleep and snoring loudly. I stopped and watched him for a moment. As I listened to him snore, I knew that this was an opportunity we needed to take advantage of.

I ran back across the dam, told the other boys of Red's security breach, and discussed the possibilities with them. Of course, we quickly came up with a plan.

Ted and I walked back to the campfire where Red was still sound asleep. I quietly picked up Red's best fishing rod and reeled the line in to the bank. Then I cut the hook and weight off and handed the end of the line to Ted, the older and bigger Estep brother. Ted ran back across the dam with the end of the line as I held the pole and reeled off as much line as he needed to get to the other side.

When I felt that there was no more line going out, I gently set the brake on the reel and returned to where the other boys were waiting.

Once we were all ready, it was my job to go wake Red so that the fun could begin.

I approached the campfire noisily this time, but, seeing that it had no effect on Pete's slumbering father, I walked up and grabbed his arm and shook his whole body.

"Red!" I said loudly. "Wake up! The fish ain't biting and Pete and me are ready to go."

He opened his eyes.

"I'm going back over to help the other boys with our stuff. We'll be ready to go when I get back."

I turned and walked back over the dam. As I got to the edge of the firelight, I could see Red slowly climbing out of his recliner. I raced through the dark back to Pete and the Esteps.

Ted had wrapped the line of Red's fishing pole around his hand and was standing out in the pasture about ten feet back from the edge of the water. At this time, Ted was about nineteen years old. He was short, but was an athletic 220 pounds and a pretty fair football player. We all waited patiently for Red to tug on the line.

Sure enough, it finally happened. Ted walked slowly toward the water, allowing Red to reel in the line, while Dale, Pete, and I all watched. When Ted reached the edge of the water, he stopped and allowed the line to go taut around his hand. Within a few seconds the line had tightened and Ted set the hook. He gave two tugs on the line, then took off at a dead run back out through the pasture.

Suddenly, from across the lake we heard a loud yell. "Holy…!"

We all tried to keep our laughter down, though I doubt Red would have heard us. After all, he had hooked a state-record fish.

As Ted ran back through the pasture, we could hear the brake on Red's reel squealing. Then, Ted stopped and let Pete's dad pull him back to the shoreline, giving just enough resistance to let Red know that he was still on the line. After he reached the edge of the water, Ted took off again out into the pasture. He must have repeated this process for about fifteen minutes. We could hear Red huffing and puffing on the other side of the lake, trying to reel in his huge fish. It was the fight of a lifetime for Red.

At last, Ted began to tire after being pulled to the shoreline for the tenth time or so. On the last time, he ran as far and as fast as he could back into the grass and, the moment Red started reeling him back, Ted popped the line just as if it had been broken by a fish.

When the line popped, all we heard from the other side of the lake was moaning and gasping, then a lot of yelling and cursing, and then the sound of things breaking.

We hurriedly carried our gear back over to the other side of the lake. Upon reaching the campfire, we found Red sitting on the edge of the reclining chair with his head buried in his hands.

"Red?" I said. "We heard you yelling over here. Did you have a fish on your line?"

Red looked up and began to tell us, quite passionately, about how he had just hung the biggest fish in the whole state of Oklahoma. We couldn't help but laugh. But he failed to find any humor in the story and looked at us in puzzlement.

Pete finally decided to have mercy on him. "Your giant fish was actually Ted yanking on the other end of your line," he said. "He was across the lake jerking and running around in the pasture with the line tied around his hand the whole time."

But Red didn't believe him. Pete's story only made him more upset and more emphatic that he had indeed hooked the big one. He claimed that he could hear it flopping in the water. In the end, he called us all liars and adamantly insisted that he did too have a big fish on the line.

Even years later, whenever anyone would tell a story about a huge catfish, Red would argue and swear that he did have a huge catfish on his line that night at Stroud Lake. It was one time that Pete and I *didn't* get the blame we deserved, because Red genuinely believed his own story. In the end, Red never did give up on his fish story, and tenaciously maintained it even up to the day he passed away.

ᗮGeorgie the Parrotᗮ

When Pete and I were about fourteen years old we frequented the pool hall in Geary. The pool hall was where all the farmers and ranchers hung out when they brought their wives into town to do the weekly shopping. While their wives shopped, the men would gather in the back room and play cards or dominoes.

The pool hall was owned by Mr. Sisney, an older man who had come to Oklahoma from California many years before. When Mr. Sisney arrived in Geary he had brought along a small, green parrot that he called "Georgie." Georgie was famous among the local kids in town because he could talk and say short phrases.

Now Georgie had accumulated a fairly large vocabulary of curse words, and one of his favorite phrases to blurt out was, "You're a d--n Okie!" I guess he had learned that phrase back in California as an insult to all the poor folks from Oklahoma who had moved out to California during the Dust Bowl many years before.

All the young men used to hang around in front of the pool hall during the summers. Most of the time the front doors of the pool hall would be left wide open and Georgie could be heard cursing at people or whistling at girls outside as they passed by on the street. Some people in town still hadn't discovered that there was a parrot in the pool hall. We always got a kick out of seeing the shock on people's faces when they would hear Georgie cursing at them from inside as they passed, not knowing that the voice yelling at them was merely a parrot.

It was late spring, and school was about to let out for the summer. Pete and I had been trying to collect enough bait to go fishing at one of the local ponds. We were in the kitchen with Mary gathering supplies for our fishing trip when Red came in through the back door and sullenly plopped down in a chair at the table. After a few seconds, he spoke.

"Mr. Sisney passed away," he reported dryly.

Pete and I had both liked the old guy, mostly because he would let us sneak inside the pool hall and play pool for free. Kids under sixteen weren't normally allowed inside. I think he just wanted to keep us off the streets and out of trouble…not that Pete and I were ever involved in any trouble.

Once inside the pool hall, we would tease Georgie. And Pete was constantly trying to teach him new curse words. Pete had always said that he would love to have Georgie as a pet. Personally, I was afraid of what Pete might teach him if he actually had full-time access to the bird.

"What's going to happen to Georgie?" Pete asked quickly.

"I don't know," answered Red. "Maybe they'll give him to the zoo or somewhere they keep animals. They'll have to do something with him because those things might live fifty years."

This began Pete's relentless begging and whining to Mary to let him and me keep the parrot.

"We'll be responsible for everything," he said. "We promise he won't be any trouble. We'll clean his cage, feed and water him, and do everything possible to keep him happy."

Mary just quietly responded that she would think about it.

Of course, Pete never mentioned that Georgie had a problem with cursing. But we didn't think it would matter much, anyway. After all, she had heard Red unload on Pete and me plenty of times.

Eventually, it was Red who got fed up with hearing Pete whine.

"Why not just let them have the parrot," he told Mary. "He's just like Pete, anyway. He's a sloppy eater and has a bad attitude."

A couple weeks later, Pete and I were the proud owners of Georgie, the parrot. At first we thought it was extremely cool to own a parrot, but it wasn't long until we figured out that there was more to it than we had expected. Georgie was used to a life of ease, hanging out indoors on his perch eating various fruits and seeds.

First of all, we were required to locate, and pay for, all of Georgie's food. We quickly learned that a half-pound parrot can eat about four times its body weight in a week. Plus, Georgie could deliver a terrible bite that would bring blood if you trespassed into his territory without permission. In the span of a month, neither Pete nor I had been able to teach Georgie a single thing. It was all we could do to keep him fed and watered while still getting all our other chores done.

On top of all of this, we found that Georgie must have been grieving Mr. Sisney's death. Our talking parrot had become totally, utterly mute. He hadn't spoken a single word in the entire month that we had owned him. We were concerned that Georgie missed Mr. Sisney so much that he might never speak again.

In the weeks following, Georgie kind of warmed up to Pete and me. He stopped biting us when we entered his perching area and would jump onto our hands if we held them out to him. He was required to stay in an outbuilding, but Pete and I would carry him around the yard and sometimes into the house. As time went on, I managed to get Georgie to take single sunflower seeds from between my fingers without biting me in the process.

One day while I was playing alone with Georgie, I took a huge chance. I placed a single sunflower seed on my tongue to see if Georgie would take it off my tongue without biting me. Sure enough, Georgie plucked the single seed from my tongue without a problem. Over the next few days, and without Pete's knowledge, I trained Georgie to take a sunflower seed from between my lips. The process made it look as if Georgie were giving me a kiss. I finally decided to share this new trick with Pete.

It was late in the evening and we had finished all our chores. We were both just killing time in the little building where Georgie lived. I walked over to the perch where Georgie sat and he jumped out onto my extended hand. I turned to Pete.

"Hey, watch what I've taught Georgie to do," I said. Then, without letting Pete see, I placed a sunflower seed between my lips and said, "Georgie, give me a kiss." I leaned forward and Georgie took the sunflower seed from between my tightly clenched lips. It would have looked to anyone watching like Georgie had given me a peck on the lips.

"That's cool!" Pete said, as usual. "Let me try it!"

Pete took Georgie from my hand and immediately started trying to get Georgie to give him a kiss, with no results. Georgie just ignored him.

As this continued, I kept taunting Pete. "I don't think Georgie likes you," I would say.

This little trick of mine went on for about two weeks without Pete finding out about it. But I was starting to feel guilty because Pete was beginning to get a complex that Georgie really didn't like him. One afternoon I finally gave in to my conscience and showed Pete the secret of getting Georgie to kiss me. Of course, once Pete tried the sunflower seed trick, Georgie quickly gave him a kiss as well.

After a few more tries, Pete grabbed a handful of sunflower seeds and said, "Let's go show Mary!"

I accompanied Pete into the house where Pete demonstrated the new trick to Mary, being careful not to let her see the sunflower seed.

"He won't give you a kiss," Pete told her. "He's lived in the pool hall so long, he's just not used to women."

Eventually, Mary got Georgie to sit on her hand, but she could not coax him into giving her a kiss and simply gave up. Pete and I took him back outside.

We had owned Georgie for about four months now. We had taught him a few more tricks, but none as cool as the kissing trick. And, still, Georgie had not uttered a word, cursing or otherwise.

One afternoon after milking time, Pete and I were playing with Georgie in the house. There was a tap at the back door and we heard a small, frail voice say, "Is anybody home?"

It was the preacher's wife, Miss Lilly—a petite, thin woman and longtime friend of Mary. Pete and I knew from past experience that when the preacher's wife showed up we were supposed to excuse ourselves and go back outside so that the women could gossip in peace. Thus, we gathered up Georgie and headed for the back door.

As we met Miss Lilly in the hallway, she exclaimed, "Oh, what a cute little parrot!"

Pete and I stopped, and the conversation turned to the bird. We were answering questions about the parrot when Miss Lilly stuck out her hand and Georgie accepted her invitation. She walked back into the kitchen with the bird on her clenched fist and approached Mary, who was sitting at the table drinking coffee.

As she walked, Miss Lilly was bombarding Georgie with, "Polly want a cracker?" and other similarly ridiculous phrases in an attempt to get Georgie to say something. But, as he had been for months, Georgie remained utterly silent.

Mary must have seen Miss Lilly's growing frustration with Georgie's failure to speak. "Georgie will give you a kiss if you ask him to," she suggested.

Immediately, Miss Lilly puckered her lips and leaned down toward Georgie, saying, "Give me a kiss, Georgie."

Pete and I smirked at each other. She didn't know the secret. But, much to our amazement, it looked as if Georgie was truly about to give Miss Lilly a kiss!

What we didn't know was that as Miss Lilly had puckered her lips, she had exposed a large black mole just inside the bottom of her lip on the left side. Well, you guessed it. When she inadvertently showed Georgie her mole, he mistook it for a sunflower seed and reached out and bit Miss Lilly right on the lip.

The preacher's wife screamed in terror and grabbed Georgie around the body with her hand, squeezing him and shrieking like a banshee. All the squeezing and screaming scared poor Georgie, and only made him clamp down harder on her lip. After about three spins in a circle, and with great effort, Miss Lilly finally managed to pull Georgie loose from her lip. Blood was spewing from her face.

Once he had escaped Miss Lilly's death clutch, Georgie took to the air and flew two full circles around the kitchen, finally landing on top of the refrigerator, shaking his whole body and ruffling his feathers. Then, at the top of his voice, he yelled, "You're a d--n Okie!"

Pete and I only got to keep Georgie about two more weeks after that, just long enough for Mary to find him a new home.

When I got older I heard of a bar in Okarche that had a small, green parrot that cussed like a sailor. I always assumed it had to be Georgie.

ঌThe Lake Houseঌ

It was late spring. All the trees were full with green leaves and flowers were blooming everywhere. It was a perfect day. Pete and I were leaning back against the wall of the cellar that had been built after all of us had almost been blown away by a tornado. We had finished our morning chores and were basking in the sun while making plans for what we would do the rest of the day.

Just then, Red came by on his way from the milk barn back to the house. "What do you boys have planned for the day?"

"Nothing special," we replied.

"You want to make two hundred dollars?" he asked.

We didn't take the bait. Red had tricked us before. Once we had gone into the pool hall to retrieve him for Mary. As we stood there beside the domino table, Red turned to us and asked, "You boys want to make a half dollar real slick?"

"Sure," we replied. "How?"

Red just sat back in his chair and laughed as he said, "Grease it."

All of the old guys sitting around the table got a big kick out of his joke and laughed out loud. Somehow Pete and I missed the humor. I could just remember thinking that we had been publicly labeled as a couple of gullible morons. So, for Red to ask us if we wanted to make two hundred dollars, we knew there had to be a catch. We left his question unanswered.

He was obviously perturbed at our lack of respect as he continued to stare at us lying on the ground. "Well, do you want to make two hundred dollars or not?" he repeated.

Finally, we relented. "OK, what do we have to do?"

"All you have to do is tear down that old house that's down on the Lake place."

Red had recently bought a farm about two miles north of where we lived from an older lady named Lake. Her husband had passed away and I'm not sure she knew how to drive, so she had moved into town and left the old farmhouse deserted.

Now, for someone to tell two sixteen-year-old farm boys like Pete and me that they could actually get paid for tearing something up was nothing short of a dream come true. But we didn't want to seem too enthusiastic, so we played it cool.

Still, daydreams immediately began to flash through my mind of what I might be able to do with a hundred dollars. Visions of fast cars and pretty girls danced in my head. One hundred dollars in Geary, Oklahoma, at that time would virtually put one in the same category of wealth as Howard Hughes. On the other hand, it gave me chills to think about what manner of evil Pete would be capable of with a hundred dollars at his disposal. I returned to reality and the task at hand.

"When can we start?" I asked.

"I'll get some hammers, saws, and crowbars and follow you boys up there," said Red. "You can take the truck."

It was about eight o'clock in the morning. Pete and I scrambled to get a lunch packed and some jugs of water and anything else we thought we might need to accomplish the job. Then we jumped into the old truck and headed north to the Lake house.

On the way, we discussed what we were going to do with the money. Pete was quitting school and moving to California to become a beach bum. I didn't voice it, but I knew Pete didn't have to move to California to be a bum. Geary was already home to quite a number of expert bums.

Soon we arrived at the Lake house and began to examine the job we had agreed to do. We found it easy to stand out in front of the house and tear it down verbally. Red's words echoed in our heads, "All you have to do is tear down that old house…."

It seemed so simple. Standing there, we verbally tore all the shingles off the top, verbally took all the rafters down, and verbally tore each wall down starting at the south end. We wanted to tear down the south wall first so that all the dirt and debris wouldn't blow all over us and get in our eyes. In the span of mere minutes we had verbally torn the house down all the way to the foundation. Nothing was left but to spend our two hundred dollars. Easy. Of course, neither of us had yet so much as touched a hammer or crowbar, but we had vision.

Red came driving in on the dirt road that led to the house. He got out and started unloading all the tools we would need to do the job. As he unloaded, he commented, "Now, you boys don't get paid until that house is totally torn down to the foundation and all the lumber is stacked beneath that old elm tree over there." He pointed to a big elm tree standing about thirty yards south of the old house. "And when you're finished, each of you will get a crisp, new, one hundred-dollar bill."

I looked at Pete. He was looking at me. This job was starting to seem like a lot of work. There had been no mention of lumber stacking in the initial negotiation, and including such a detail now sure didn't seem fair. But neither of us ever argued with Red, except about fishing.

"Now, do you boys understand what you're supposed to do?" Red asked, winding down his description of the job.

"Yes. All we gotta do is tear down this house to the rock foundation and stack all the lumber under that old elm tree."

"That's right," replied Red. Then he got into his truck and left.

Pete and I gathered our tools, climbed onto the roof of the house, and started tearing shingles off. It was dirty, nasty, backbreaking work. After about two hours of bending over and pulling off shingles, we had to have a break. We climbed down and sat in the shade of the elm tree and discussed recruiting some help. We thought about getting Ted and Dale Estep to help us. We could lie and tell them we were only getting a hundred dollars and that they could have fifty. We sat there for about an hour without moving.

When we finally decided to get back to work, we started on the inside walls because it was getting to be the hot part of the day and we didn't want to be on the roof in the sun. We each chose different rooms to start in. Pete was in what appeared to be the kitchen and I was in another small room next to it. The walls had been covered with some kind of plaster that had been put over small wooden boards. The boards were old, well-cured, and extremely tough. I could hear Pete moaning and groaning as he beat around on things in the next room.

A few minutes later, Pete called me in to help him. He had managed to pry a long board loose from the wall and he wanted me to help him pull on it. The board seemed to run the full length of the kitchen wall. Pete and I both took hold of the board and began to pull with all our strength. Finally, it popped and came flying loose along with lots of dust and plaster.

But there was something else. Out of the wall, all along the length of the board, came about two gallons of honeycomb and ten thousand angry honeybees. We were immediately covered by the swarm. Both of us scrambled for the door, fighting and swatting at bees all the way. After we had run about fifty yards and were basically free of the bees, we stopped to survey the damage.

We counted whelps from the stings on each other's backs. I don't remember exactly how many there were, but it was a lot.

Pete looked at me in disgust. "This job stinks! I quit!"

Pete and I both knew that Red had a strong philosophy regarding work ethic. He had a little saying that he would constantly recite to Pete and me when we worked with him:

> *Once a task you have begun,*
> *Do not leave it 'til it's done.*
> *Be it big or be it small,*
> *Do it right or not at all.*

I looked at Pete. We both knew that we had agreed to do the job and we couldn't quit just because things got tough. We ambled over to the elm tree and sat down again, depressed about the deal we had made with Red.

"What are we going to do about those bees?" Pete asked. "We can't go back in there or they'll sting us to death."

"They'll calm down after a while," I said. "Then we can go back in and throw a can of diesel on them and kill them." Pete didn't seem satisfied with my suggestion.

Leaning against the big elm tree, I could tell that Pete's mind had begun to think about how we could get the job done without actually working. I sat under the tree, while Pete wandered aimlessly back toward the old house.

Between the tree and the house there was an old cement cellar with a sheet metal door covering it. I watched as Pete's curiosity got the best of him and he walked over to the metal door and flopped it open onto the ground. He stood peering down into the cellar for a moment, and then disappeared down the stairs.

A couple of minutes elapsed with no noises or activity from the cellar. Then, suddenly, Pete's head protruded above the cellar doorway. His eyes were wide with excitement and he had a big smile on his face.

"You ain't gonna believe what's down here!" he said.

I walked over to the cellar door, wondering what Pete might have found. My thoughts ranged from kettles of gold coins to dead bodies. Whatever it was, I could see that it had made a huge impression on Pete, and to me that was a bit frightening.

As I approached the doorway, I looked down inside. I could see that the floor was damp with moisture and, through the dim light, I could see the bottom half of Pete's legs at the back of the cellar. As I walked down the steps, I saw that he was standing in front of a set of shelves. Coming up beside him, I looked here and there, trying to find what had impressed him so much.

At first, I didn't see anything that I found especially extraordinary. There were just some old jars; all of them covered with dust, and some of them filled with rotten fruit or vegetables. Other jars had been broken and their pieces were scattered along the shelves.

But, as my eyes adjusted to the light, I finally discovered what Pete had found. There, in faded orange letters on the sides of two boxes sitting on the top shelf were the words: *Danger! Dynamite*. And just to the side of these boxes were two smaller boxes with the same faded lettering that read: *Danger! Blasting Caps*.

I turned to Pete. "Do you know what we can do with this?"

It was one of the few times that Pete was completely speechless. All he could do was stare at the boxes with his mouth half open and nod his head up and down.

We had personally witnessed the use of dynamite a few years earlier when the county workers had used it to blow some gypsum rock out of the way during road construction. They had cleared out the rocks for a new bridge that crossed the creek about three miles east of the Lake house.

Mr. Lake had once been the county commissioner. We guessed that he had purchased the dynamite years earlier for some roadwork. Evidently, he had not used all of it, and had stored the remainder in his cellar. It seemed that neither Mrs. Lake nor anyone else knew it was down here. Whatever the case, Pete and I were now standing in front of a fairly large stash of explosives.

The old boxes were almost totally rotten from the moisture. Pete and I wrangled the first one down onto the floor and opened it up. Inside were a number of small brownish sticks made of rolled paper. Each stick was about twelve inches long and an inch in diameter. The dynamite was so old that some of the paper had dissolved and the whitish-gray powder inside them had become wet and had settled to the bottom of the box. The remainder of the sticks also felt as if they had a lot of moisture in them, because they had small beads of sticky goop leaking from the paper.

After our initial examination, Pete turned to me and said, "You think this stuff will still work?"

"I don't know," I replied. "It looks pretty damp."

But there was never a thought in our minds that we wouldn't try the dynamite. We had to at least see if it would work. There were a number of possibilities on how we might do a test run, but in the end I suggested that we blow up the bees.

We snuck back into the house and did a reconnaissance of the bees. The biggest part of the hive was still in the wall, so most of the bees had returned to the hole in the wall that Pete and I had created when we ripped off the board. We made a plan to take a stick of dynamite and place it against the wall on the outside of the house opposite where the bees were in the kitchen. That way, we reasoned, we could blow up the bees without disturbing them again and thus prevent more bee stings.

We returned to the cellar and retrieved a stick of dynamite. We carried it to the porch, along with a blasting cap and the directions contained in the blasting cap box. One of the written instructions stated that if a full charge was not needed, the stick of dynamite could be cut into two or three smaller pieces. Pete and I decided that half a stick would probably be sufficient to kill a nest of bees. Plus, we weren't even sure it would work.

Using my pocket knife, we cut the stick of dynamite into two pieces. Then, just as the picture and instructions directed, we inserted the blasting cap. Next, we positioned ourselves on the outside wall of the house directly opposite the beehive. We took a shingle that we had torn off the roof and nailed both ends to the wall, forming an envelope at just the height the bees would be in the house. Finally, we slipped the half-stick of dynamite into the shingle envelope which held it firmly against the wall.

It seemed that Pete's thinking and mine were on the same page. We set about our business with very little talking. We were both ready for some action and to see what would be the result of our first stick of dynamite.

We led the wires from the blasting cap to a distance of about thirty yards from the front porch of the old house. Then we discussed how to set off the charge. We decided to use the battery from the truck and discussed taking it out and carrying it over to the blasting cap wires. We could then touch the wires to the battery and set off the dynamite. But, as usual, Pete was too lazy take out the battery and lug it over to where we were. So, he decided it would be simpler and faster to just drive the truck over to where we were with the wires.

Pete drove the truck up to the end of the wires, allowing room so that we had enough slack in the wires to get to the battery. This put the truck about twenty-five yards from the house.

Finally, with great anticipation, we opened the hood of the truck and retrieved the wires from the ground. Since we had no idea what the outcome would be, or if it would even work, Pete allowed me to do the honors of touching the wires to the battery.

I had stripped and cleaned the ends of both wires, leaving about an inch of shiny new wire on each side. I placed the first wire, which was red, against the positive side of the battery. Then, I slowly started toward the negative side with the black wire. As my hand approached the battery I was hoping that this was going to be as cool as we thought it might be.

Kaboom! The sound was loud, but not as loud as I had expected. White smoke billowed from the windows of the old house, but there was not a bee to be seen. We quickly ran up to the porch and pushed our way inside to the kitchen where the beehive had been. There, before our eyes, was a perfectly round hole about six feet in diameter. The hole was so perfect that it looked as if someone had come into the house with a jigsaw and cut a circular hole in the wall to remove the bees. Pete and I were now certified experts in the field of demolition.

As we contemplated how effective and efficient the use of dynamite could be, we came up with a simple equation: dynamite placed in a strategic location, minus physical labor, equaled two hundred dollars. We quickly went to work putting our equation into action.

Pete and I were no novices. We had once watched a building being demolished on television. The dynamite had been carefully placed within the building so that when it was set off, the building simply settled gently onto the ground in a pile of dust. Of course, this was before those pesky don't-try-this-at-home disclaimers. But it wouldn't have mattered. In our minds, Pete and I were now professionals.

We immediately began to rig the house for destruction. We went down to the cellar and brought up the entire case of dynamite. We began to place sticks in each corner of every room and wire them together. At this point, our high school math class came in handy. There were four rooms plus a kitchen and a porch. We figured a stick in each corner of the house and a few more under the floor along the rock foundation for good measure. Eventually, we agreed that twenty-four sticks of dynamite would do the job nicely.

Pete and I were both in full demolition mode when an old man came walking into the house. In our fierce concentration, neither of us had heard him drive up. It was Shorty Petticrew. Shorty was a man we knew from the community who used to work on Mr. Lake's road crew when Mr. Lake had been county commissioner. He was also a little nosy and liked to gather information to feed the local gossip.

Shorty walked into the house while Pete and I were bent down in a corner putting dynamite stick number fourteen into place. As Pete and I worked intently, Shorty relayed the story of how he had bumped into Red at the local farmer's cooperative. Red had told him about hiring us to tear down the old Lake house and Shorty had just dropped in to check on our progress. While he stood jabbering away, he finally noticed what Pete and I had in our hands.

He stammered and stuttered for a moment, then managed to get out a few words. "That…uh… looks like dynamite you boys got there."

"It *is* dynamite," Pete responded without even bothering to look up. "We're gonna blow this old house up."

Shorty stood in the doorway of what used to be the living room, surveying the four sticks of dynamite we had already placed in the corners. I took my eyes off of him for a second and when I looked up again he was gone. I walked to the front door of the house to look for him, but neither Shorty nor his truck was anywhere to be seen. I returned to the kitchen.

"Where did Shorty go?" Pete asked.

"I don't know," I answered. "I guess he had better things to do."

After about two hours everything seemed to be in place. Pete and I walked back through the house, checking every wire and blasting cap to make sure everything was rigged properly. Afterward, we went back out to the elm tree and rested while we discussed how surprised Red would be that we had torn down the house in less than a day. The money would soon be ours.

Of course, there was the matter of having to stack the lumber under the tree. But we figured that wouldn't be a problem. Once the house had gently collapsed into a pile like we had seen on television, we would simply gather the boards, pull a few nails, and stack it all under the elm.

After we caught our breath we walked over to the old truck. We had run the wire from each stick of dynamite to the main wire that led out of the house and off the porch. We had also attached about thirty extra yards of wire onto the end of the main wire to give us more distance between us and the house. We were now about fifty yards from the house.

Pete moved the truck to the end of the blasting cap wire. As we raised the hood I wondered whether we were far enough away. I questioned Pete about it.

"Look," he said calmly. "All this is gonna do is knock the support out from under the house and the walls are gonna fall right where they're at in a big pile of boards."

"OK," I said, shrugging my shoulders.

Pete stuck the red wire to the positive side of the battery and started toward the negative side with the black wire. But before he even reached the post, a small arc of electricity jumped out from it to the end of the black wire. The charge set off all twenty-four sticks of dynamite simultaneously. It was literally earth-shaking. It sent the whole house into the air about two hundred feet and then blew it outwards in every direction about a quarter of a mile. Unfortunately, when the house went, so did the foundation. Both the house and the foundation erupted into ten million pieces. The foundation was blown into softball-sized chunks, while the boards from the house were splintered into pieces not longer than two feet and were scattered across an alfalfa field that surrounded the house.

Some of the rocks from the foundation went skyward. Pete and I watched them until they started falling back to earth around us. We scrambled for cover in the truck. As I hunkered down in the floor of the pickup, I could see a huge mushroom-shaped cloud that had been carried by the wind about a mile into the air. I figured people five miles away in Greenfield could probably see it. I was just hoping that Red and Mary couldn't see it from home.

Since this was the early 1960's, most people were really paranoid about atomic weapons. I could just imagine phones ringing off the wall as Miss Margaret and Miss Pearl informed everyone that the Russians had made a pre-emptive nuclear missile strike near Greenfield, Oklahoma.

Pete and I huddled in the truck as sand, dirt, splintered boards, and pieces of rock fell to the ground. Once everything had settled, Pete opened the door and stepped out to stare at the bare, scorched ground where the Lake house had once stood. Then, as if nothing special had taken place, Pete looked at me and commented plainly, "Man, that stuff works good, don't it?"

All I could think about was how we were going to gather all the pieces of rock and debris. It would take all summer.

"What are we gonna do with all the rocks, boards, shingles, and stuff?" I asked.

"Simple," Pete replied. "We'll just pile it up and burn it. We'll probably be done by sundown and we can have our money by tomorrow night." The next night just happened to be Saturday.

We piled up everything we could manage to gather and burned it. But there were so many miniscule pieces that it was impossible to collect them all. As usual, Pete had a plan.

"Look," he began. "Red won't come over here for a few days. We'll just tell him that we stacked the boards like he said and that a storm must have hit the board pile after we stacked it and scattered it everywhere."

It was not quite sundown when we made it back to the house. Pete and I were once again leaning against the cellar when Red emerged from the barn.

"How much of that old house did you boys get torn down?" he asked.

"All of it," Pete answered proudly. "And we want our money before tomorrow night."

"There ain't no way you boys could have torn that house down in a day," snapped Red. He must have trusted me more than Pete because he turned to me and looked me straight in the face. "Cody, did you boys tear that entire house down?"

"Yes, sir," I said apprehensively. "The Lake house is no longer standing."

Red squinted at us. "You boys get in the truck," he said firmly. "We're gonna see what kind of job you've done."

"Uh," I stammered, "I'm too tired to ride back over there right now."

Red looked at Pete lying on the ground. "Get in the truck!" he said to Pete. Then he turned to me. "You too!"

Walking toward the truck, I mumbled to Pete, "I'm riding by the door."

As we left the driveway, I wondered what would happen when we got there. I couldn't believe that no one had called Red or Mary about the explosion yet.

"What did you boys do with all the boards?" Red asked as he drove.

"We stacked them under the elm tree just like you told us," Pete said. This was partially true, as we had stacked some wood under the tree, but Pete left out the part where the boards had been blown into two-foot long splinters.

It was getting dark when Red drove through the gate that led to the Lake house. As he turned into the drive, he could plainly see that the house was no longer there. He stopped the truck about a hundred yards from where the house should have been and stared in amazement at the brown square of dirt where the house once stood.

"How did you boys get that house down so quick?" he asked in amazement.

"Does it make any difference?" Pete replied brazenly. "The house is gone and we want our two hundred dollars."

I wasn't so optimistic. I was grasping the door handle in preparation for a quick escape. But Red still hadn't quite put everything together yet.

Red pulled the truck closer to where the house had been. As he did, small pieces of rock, shingles, and board splinters became visible in the dirt roadway. I could hear Red's breathing become deeper and more pronounced. I thought he might be hyperventilating. When we finally turned directly toward the house, Red turned on the headlights of the truck to get a better look. He could now plainly see what we had done. He knew that we'd blown up the house; he just didn't know how.

A few moments later, the Lake property experienced its second explosion of the day. This one was from Red.

"You two crazy, ignorant...!"

As I pulled the handle and jumped out of the truck to run I could hear him cursing at us and suggesting that our births had occurred outside the bonds of marriage. But his voice soon faded because I was already out of range and into the trees across the road. I guess, at that point, my life was worth more to me than two hundred dollars.

Years later, while serving in the military in Vietnam, I learned that only the slightest spark of electricity could have set off all that dynamite at once with Pete and me still inside the house. I guess we're lucky to still be alive.

ꙮSneaking Outꙮ

Pete's grandmother on Mary's side was now in her eighties. She was an amazing lady. I could never believe how many books she had read, or that she had never owned a television. The knowledge she had acquired was frightening.

She had moved into town years earlier and lived in a large two-story house. Her health was failing and she needed constant care. To this end, family members would take turns staying at Grandma's house and watching her. At present, it was Mary's turn and she was in town taking care of her mother.

Pete and I had just finished our chores and walked back into the house. It seemed so empty without Mary rustling around. We admitted to each other that we kind of missed her yelling at us and telling us to go do stuff.

Shortly, Red came in. Just as he was coming down the hallway, the phone rang. Pete grabbed the receiver and Red was immediately standing at his side. Pete said "yes" a few times, and then handed the phone to Red. After a short conversation, he hung up and turned to us.

"You boys get ready," he said. "We're going to town to stay the night with Mary."

This was great news for Pete and me. Going to town was like a vacation for us, and we always stayed packed and ready to go.

When we got to town, we found that Mary had fixed us all a big supper. Red and Mary talked of her mother's worsening condition and seemed rather concerned about it.

After supper, Red and Mary partnered against Pete and me in a game of pitch. Red kept a close eye on us because we were prone to cheating. Once the game was over, Red looked at us and said, "You boys get upstairs and go to bed. We need to be back home early in the morning to do the milking."

Pete and I went upstairs where there were two large beds. We each had our own bed with lots of quilts and extra space. I went over to the window and opened it so that the cool summer breeze could blow through the room.

We lay back on our beds and were really getting comfortable. We probably could have fallen asleep in a matter of moments, except that we heard something. It was the sound of voices. From across a small open field behind the house we could hear people screaming and laughing. We jumped from our beds and ran to the window. There, across the field, were about twenty of our friends, both male and female, playing tennis beneath the lights at the town tennis court. These were all kids from school that we hadn't been able to see all summer. Suddenly, we desperately needed to be over there with them.

"Let's go ask Red if we can go over to the tennis courts for a while," I suggested.

"What a stupid idea," Pete replied, rolling his eyes. "He knows us too well. He's not gonna let us go over there."

I knew Pete was right. We watched our friends for a few more minutes, especially the girls.

"Well, what are we gonna do?" I asked in frustration. "We can't just sit here."

"No," said Pete. "We're gonna have a jailbreak!" He jumped to his feet. "Let's get these sheets off the bed."

We started pulling sheets off the bed and tying them into large knots to make a rope long enough that it would reach the ground. It was one of our usual, simple plans. We would tie five or six sheets together, secure them to the largest bed, and slide down the sheets to the ground.

Finally we got all the sheets tied together and lowered them to the ground. Of course, as with most of our plans, I was the one chosen to have the first try. This time it was supposedly due to my being smaller and lighter than Pete. I would simply take hold of the rope, place my feet against the wall of the house, and walk to the bottom.

I was totally out of the window when I discovered that I was about twenty feet above the ground. I started to climb down the rope, but my feet slipped and I went crashing into the wall of the house and slid down the sheets. The boards on the house tore the skin off my knuckles as I slid down. I squealed as I burnt my way down the rope to the ground, finally crashing into some crepe myrtle bushes. I examined my knuckles and knees. Cutoff jeans don't offer much protection.

I looked up at Pete. As usual, he had found my pain quite entertaining and was in a fit of laughter at my plight. It took me a while, but I finally convinced him that it wasn't all that bad and that he should throw our shoes out and come down after me. Pete took his turn with the same result: bruised knees, skinned knuckles, and a large thud at the end that snapped crepe myrtle bushes in a cloud of dust and branches.

Meanwhile, unknown to us, Mary had heard banging on the wall and screaming from outside. She had awakened Red and had managed to convince him that burglars were outside and that they were attempting to break in and kill us all. After some amount of pleading, Red agreed to go out and take a look. On his way outside, he grabbed a baseball bat that was behind the door.

Meanwhile, Pete and I were just getting our wits about us and our shoes tied, when Pete whispered, "Hey, I think I hear something in those bushes."

Then, just as I was getting my last shoelace tied, Pete turned and ran completely over the top of me. "Run! There's a big guy in the bushes with a baseball bat!"

Terrified, we fought our way through the crepe myrtle bushes toward the back door of the house. We burst through the door and ran straight through the kitchen and into the hallway where we met Red, who was still in his underwear, coming from the front. He had seen us outside, but, failing to realize it was us, he had concluded that there were, in fact, intruders.

He had come back inside and abandoned his baseball bat, intending to find better weaponry. We, on the other hand, didn't know that it was Red we saw outside and we assumed that he had just gotten out of bed.

As I stood wondering to myself why we hadn't just snuck downstairs and out the front door to begin with, Pete blurted out, "There's someone out there!"

"I know," said Red, who didn't know we had been outside and thought we had just run down from upstairs. "Be quiet."

We were all three now getting ready to confront the burglars. Red snuck down to the hall closet and grabbed an old break-open twelve-gauge shotgun. Rummaging through some boxes, he found a single shell. Then, the three of us went out the front door and headed slowly toward the crepe myrtle bushes. As we inched around the corner of the house, the white glow of sheets hanging from the upstairs bedroom came into view.

Red was still puzzling over the sheets, when Pete felt the need to warn Red about the burglars. "Be careful," Pete cautioned. "One of them has a baseball bat!"

Immediately, Red lowered his gun and turned to stare at Pete. "Now, how do *you* know one of them has a baseball bat?"

Then, suddenly, it all came together and everyone realized what had happened.

"You two..!"

Pete and I figured a guy with a shotgun was more dangerous than a guy with a baseball bat, so we ran.

❧Blind Sections☙

Almost every family in the community had a small dairy, and part of the annual ritual was to put up some kind of winter feed for the dairy cattle. Red had always stuck to the old way of doing things when it came to farming. He would plant what we called head feed, which was some sort of tall sugar cane like Sudan or Sudex.

It was about the middle of November when Red decided we needed to go and get some of this head feed to take to the dry cows that were over in the east pasture which was in the next mile section. Dry cows were the older cows that didn't have calves and were not being milked at that time.

We had left the house and traveled almost a full mile south and west to the feed patch. The head feed had been cut down in late August with a sickle blade mower. After it had been cut, Pete and I would physically pick the feed up from off the ground and put it into a machine called a "bundler." Then after the feed was bundled we would cut the head off the feed, put the heads of feed into the pickup bed and haul them to a storage bin back at the milk barn. After we cut the heads from the stalks we would stack the rest of the cane stalks into feed shocks like small tepees. This helped shed the rainwater and ice off the cane until it was removed from the field.

We arrived at the field and in no time had a full load of bundles stacked on the old green Dodge pickup truck. When I say a full load, I mean a load that was neatly stacked five feet above the cab of the truck.

After finishing our loading, Red started easing the truck out of the field to the road, driving less than a couple miles per hour. When he reached the main road he sped up a little, and was driving maybe fifteen miles per hour. We were traveling east toward the dry cow pasture. Red had settled in to his slow, quiet, methodical gaze as he drove east.

Between where we left the feed patch and the dry cow pasture there was what we called a "blind section," which meant that it was impossible to see traffic coming from the crossroad. Moreover, there were no stop signs and country people weren't accustomed to yielding. This particular blind section line had tall sunflowers growing very close to the road and along each side of it in all four directions. There had previously been a couple of vehicle crashes in the community on just such blind section line corners as the one we were approaching. And this very blind section line had, just a few weeks before, been the scene of one of these accidents. All of this was well known to Red.

Red had managed to go into a total trance in the first half mile we had traveled after we had left the field. As we got closer to the blind section I noticed he wasn't paying attention. After all, there wasn't a lot of traffic on the old dirt roads back then. Red had made the comment to Pete and me one day, "That's what I like about living in the country. I can drive out of my driveway without even looking for oncoming cars."

As we got closer to the blind intersection I began to poke Pete in the side with my elbow. Pete and I had always had a kind of mental telepathy and he began to quietly smile. When the front of the old Dodge truck had just reached the edge of the main blind intersection I quickly pointed south and as loud as I could, I let out my best James Brown scream: *"Whooooah!"* When I screamed, it of course woke Red from his hypnosis and he slammed on the brakes as hard as he could.

What happened after that is something I hadn't expected. The cane, which was stacked far above the cab of the truck, came sliding forward over it and completely covered the windshield so that

Red couldn't see the road. He spun the steering wheel with both hands, cussing a blue streak.

After a couple seconds I could feel the truck leaning, which meant we were going into the ditch. By the time the truck stopped the cane had slid all the way forward, covering the entire front of the truck. The truck was leaning almost onto its side in the ditch. The other problem that I hadn't counted on, besides the crash, was that all the cane had wedged the passenger door shut.

Pete was innocent this time, but the blows Red was throwing kept coming for both of us. Red was too close to me to get a real good punch in, although he was trying very hard to connect with a left hook.

This was long before electric windows, so I immediately reached over and began rolling down the window on the passenger side door. Pete and I both scrambled out and took off down the road. When Red managed to get out of the truck he had a claw hammer in his hand. He knew he couldn't outrun either of us because he had tried to before.

As he stood in the road he called out to us, "I'm killing you to little…" He stood in the road and called us everything but a milk cow. (This later became an inside joke between me and Pete, because I could look at him and say, "You're a milk cow," and he would burst out laughing.)

After Red calmed down he managed to get the truck out of the ditch and began to load the bundles back on the truck. After he had loaded a few bundles I guess he realized that he needed help.

"I won't kill you boys until after we get these bundles loaded, so get up here and let's get this stuff loaded back on the truck."

Now, when someone tells me that I will be put to death right after I finish a job, it tends to make me not put my full effort into it. I like to slow down a bit. Finally, we finished loading the truck for the second time and made it to the dry cow pasture. On the way to the pasture Red explained how dangerous it was for me to play a joke like that.

"Don't you ever do that to Mary," he said roughly. So I promised him I would never trick Mary like that.

It was getting dusky dark when we finished unloading and headed back to the milk barn at the house. We were approaching the same blind section where our crash had just happened. As we approached the blind section for the second time that day I nudged Pete in the side again. When I did I noticed Pete chuckling and getting the handle of the door ready as he pushed the claw hammer under the seat with his foot. As we came up on the blind section I thought, "I wonder if this will work twice in one day."

I had promised not to scare Mary. I hadn't promised not to scare Red.

"Whooooah!"

❧Hitchhiking☙

We were expecting an unusually cold winter and Red had asked Pete and me to do some work tacking pieces of thick plastic over the windows of the milk barn. The plastic on the outside would prevent everything from freezing up inside the barn. We had gathered all the necessary supplies. We had hammers, plastic, metal tacks, and some wooden slats about an inch wide.

We had just arrived at the first window of the barn when Red showed up to teach us exactly how he wanted the job done. Red cut a piece of plastic slightly larger than the window he wanted to cover and placed it in position. Then, he placed a small tack at each corner of the plastic to hold it into place. Finally, he asked Pete to hold one end of a slat that he was holding up against the plastic. He was attempting to nail the slat into place while Pete held one end of it along with the plastic.

Red began pecking at the tack with the hammer to get it started into the wood before driving it all the way into the slat. He had barely set the tack into the wood and had placed his left hand above it to brace himself for the blow he was about to strike.

Meanwhile, Pete had used his free hand to grab the sheet of plastic at the bottom in order to pull it tight and remove any wrinkles it might have. Just as Red got ready to hit the tack with a good, strong blow, the plastic slipped from the pressure that Pete was applying to it. It pulled the tack loose and, along with it, made Red's left hand slip down about four inches. This placed it directly in line with where the tack used to be. The full impact of the hammer landed squarely on Red's left thumb.

"Son…of…a…!" screamed Red, dropping the hammer and clutching his hand to his chest. I could see blood seeping from the end of his thumb.

As Red bent over clutching his hand in anguish, Pete, absentmindedly as ever, asked dumbly, "Did you smash your thumb?"

Red whirled around and stuck his throbbing blue thumb up into the air in front of Pete, "No, stupid! I'm just hitchhiking to the bathroom!"

Pete and I both burst into laughter.

Afterword

Pete and I both wanted to join the army after we graduated from high school. The day that we went to take our military physicals I met Pete out in one of the exam rooms after it was over. I asked him how his exam had gone. He turned and looked at me with excitement. "The doctor told me they would be calling me back!"

"When?" I asked quickly.

Pete just smiled his big toothy grin. "When they have wars in Braille."

I went to Vietnam and Pete went home.

So many things come to mind when I think about Red, Pete, and I working on the farm together. Sometimes, I still lie in bed at night reminiscing and laughing about all these stories. I was forty years old before I realized that most people didn't get to have all the fun that I had growing up.

Red still lived in Geary when he passed away in 1984. Mary followed him ten years later.

Pete worked in the oil and gas industry almost all of his life. Having been a state champion in wrestling like his brother, he also spent many years coaching wrestling at Geary High School.

I served with the 101st Airborne Division in Vietnam, earning two Purple Hearts and a Bronze Star. Later, I became a game warden and spent more than twenty years enforcing all the fish and game laws that I had broken as a youth. They even made me captain.

As of publication, Pete and I both still live within fifteen miles of Geary.

Cody (left) and Pete (right) in 2012.

www.ingramcontent.com/pod-product-compliance
Lightning Source LLC
Chambersburg PA
CBHW020001050426
42450CB00005B/271